Crusade and Conversion: Saracen Depiction

Annette P. Huntsman

TABLE OF CONTENTS

Acknowledgments iv

List of Abbreviations vii

Introduction 1
    Major Research Questions and Conclusions 4
    Temporal and Textual Scope 6
    Terminology 10
    Methodology: Postcolonial Theory 17
    Other Key Criticism 23
    Dissertation Outline 26

Chapter 1: *Richard Coer de Lion* and The Construction of English Identity 29
    English Language and Nationalism 34
    Cassodorien, Demon Princess of Antioch 37
    Cannibalism, Part I 50
    Cannibalism, Part II 57
    The Marble King 62
    The Chivalric Saracen: Saladin 67
    Conclusion 71

Chapter 2: Women and the Power of Conversion 73
    The Saracen Princess and Fantasy 75
    Floripas the Courteous 82
    Josian, the Distressing Damsel 89
    KT: The Princess of Tars 104
    Conclusion 120

Chapter 3: Sir Palomides, Malory's Sisyphean Saracen Knight 123
    Saracens in Arthurian Texts 126
    Palomides and Religion 139
    Palomides and Love 145
    Palomides and Gender 153
    Palomides and the Chivalric Community 159
    Conclusion 169

Conclusion 171

List of Abbreviations

RCL	Richard Coer de Lion
Bevis	Sir Bevis of Hampton
KT	The King of Tars
Morte	Morte Darthur
PG	Sir Perceval of Galles
RG	The Rise of Gawain, Nephew of Arthur
SD	Sir Degrevant
OED	Oxford English Dictionary
MED	Middle English Dictionary

Introduction

Many Middle English romances are concerned with issues of identity on the macro level of culture and religion and/or the micro level of the individual and their place in society. Against the uncertainties of shifting politics, war, and plague, these romances question what it means to be English, to be Christian, to be a man or woman, to be a king, or to be a knight. Few things help define an identity better than encountering the Other, and popular Middle English romances often incorporate anxieties and confusions of identity by using Saracens. Interestingly, Saracens can be found all over Middle English canon, from the crusade romances that send Christian knights abroad to conquer the Holy Land, to the more insular Arthurian romances. The Saracens that appear in these romances at once illuminate and confuse ideas of Middle English Christian identity. The romances also look at history, at the failed string of crusades, and wonder what it would take to be victorious in the Middle East once and for all.

Sir Isumbras[1] is one such romance that ponders identity and crusade and meditates on how the Middle East may be won. *Sir Isumbras* is the romance of a knight who has forgotten his knightly purpose as a warrior for God and is offered the choice to suffer for his sin now or when he is older (40-60). He chooses the former, and in quick order loses everything he possesses: land, money, sons, and wife. The rest of the romance is about the trials of Isumbras serving out his penance abroad before God restores him to everything he once had and more: "Thenne was the kyng Ser Ysumbras / Off more welthe thenne evere he was" (760-61). The romance is very short but manages to pack in themes of Christian duty and

---

[1] Considering the sheer number of surviving 14-15th century manuscripts that this romance appears in, *Sir Isumbras* was likely very popular. It is dated around 1320 and is found in no less than nine manuscripts (Norako "Sir Isumbras").

chivalry, *deus vult* crusading impulses, imperialism, and the wholesale Christianization of not one but three Saracen countries. Even Sir Isumbras's wife, a lady who had been abducted and forcibly married to a Sultan, takes a more aggressive role in the bloody conversions at the end of the romance when the two of them prepare to engage thirty thousand Saracens in battle, joined only by their sons (712-35). Near the end of the romance, there are three interesting lines: "Thenne three londes gunne they wynne / And crystenyd alle that was therinne, / In romaunse as men rede" (757-59). The lands are ultimately divided amongst the three sons. This means that the end of the romance not only sees the hostile takeover and conversion of a foreign pagan nation, but also sees the beginning of a Christian dynasty there as well. In other words, the romance is both crusade propaganda and a reflection on how the lands won by Christians may be kept by Christians. Furthermore, there is an element of wish fulfillment in this romance—the idea that lands lost by Christians could be regained only if Christians regained God's favor by turning their attention away from domestic matters of the world and back to God. Considering that the Crusades involved a series of failures and tenuous stalemates for Christian Europeans, this romance offers two things: an encouragement to crusade in God's service (the idea being that out of the ashes of defeat, God can grant true Christians even greater victories), and a process for turning the tides of war once and for all through conversion at sword point. The romance is a cold-blooded thought experiment that considers the possibility of forced conversion as a viable method for keeping control of the Middle East. By establishing a generational foothold in the Middle East through Isumbras's sons, and forcibly converting or killing all the inhabitants of that region, the romance argues for a long-term plan that forces the conquered lands to become Christian and thus return the lands permanently to complete Christian control. Like *Sir*

Isumbras, many of the romances I examine in this dissertation grapple with controlling and, in *Richard Coer de Lion*, literally consuming the Middle East or the Saracen Other. Conversion to Christianity, either willing or at sword point, is one common tactic in these romances, because conversion implies that Christianity is the more legitimate religion and it ostensibly tries to eliminate the Other through incorporation.

Medieval England was centuries from becoming an imperial power, but these romances may be evidence of fledgling ideas of empire and empire-building. Local conflicts between England and its neighbors of Scotland, Wales, Ireland, and France might have served as practice for future imperial endeavors, and I would argue that the literature also influences the creation and maintenance of English cultural identity. Romances can serve as thought experiments, where anxieties about the Self and Other can be played out. One of the ways a nation begins thinking of becoming a major colonial or imperial power is by having a firm grasp of who they are (or want to be) and following that realization with a missionary impulse to spread it. The ability to create a cohesive narrative, or even a fantasy, to support and spread such ideas is key. National and cultural identities are unstable; they are constantly evolving, which means that the narratives used to support those identities are also changing. Part of building an identity involves the stories we tell ourselves, both as individuals and members of a society: the heroes we admire, the villains we loathe, the values we are willing to fight and die for, and all the tiny rhetorical cues encoded in these stories. Romances, with their popular appeal, are ideal vehicles for such stories. Perhaps the textual Saracen of the Middle Ages was a convenient enemy to pit various English heroes against because he or she was foreign and not likely to be incorporated into England. The Saracen was an ideologically safe enemy to have, much safer than more local enemies. After all, the lines between

Englishman and Saracen are clearly demarcated, at least at first; there is an "us" and a "them" and the differences are so firm that they rarely challenge English identity outright. Instead, they provide a helpful contrast.

The image of the Saracen as hostile or even monstrous might be safe to write about and defeat textually because of such obvious and irreconcilable difference. However, this is not the only image of the Saracen found throughout Middle English romance. These romances may help build the foundations for identity, but they often trouble or blur those same ideas. Sometimes the differences between the Christian English knights and their Saracen enemies are negligible, or they are interchangeable with each other in terms of behavior and values. Even the Saracen princesses are sometimes whitened to resemble a European ideal of beauty. What happens if Saracens are somehow judged "worthy" through their appearance or deeds? In these cases, the romances then must grapple with how to treat a Saracen who is more alike than different. For other romances, like *Sir Isumbras*, the options of colonialism are simplified: kill or convert. Whether voluntary or at sword-point, conversion to Christianity becomes a tool of colonialism in these romances because supplanting one ideology with another is presented as a possible way to win the seemingly unwinnable Crusades, at least on parchment.

Major Research Questions and Conclusions

The purpose of this dissertation is to examine the way Middle English romances use the image of the Saracen to create English, Christian, and English/Christian identities. I study the interplay of history and literature, religions and politics, and the role that literature, specifically popular Middle English romances, played in shaping a cohesive English identity. During this project, I developed three main avenues of inquiry about identity creation and the ideological role that conversion plays as both a process and a solution to the West's frustration with the Middle East.

First, how do textual Saracens help build an English identity? One answer is through stereotyping. On the surface, Middle English romances regarding crusading or the East are about constructing identity not via sameness but through direct opposition to a threatening or foreign Other. Crusade romances are power fantasies of Christian European domination of the East. To do this, the texts often portray both sides as monolithic stereotypes: all Christians are alike, and all who are not Christian are Saracen. Romances like *Sir Isumbras* and *Richard Coer de Lion* respectively, focus a lot of attention on what it means to be a good Christian knight, and a good English king (who is then representative of all English), and creates these identities in strict opposition to the other communities in the text. Still, the answer to this question is not quite so straightforward. The *Richard Coer de Lion* romance at once holds Richard up as one of the Worthies, one of the best English kings and heroes, while also blurring the boundaries of the East/West in Richard's own nature.

My second line of inquiry is how female characters, both Christian and Saracen, are used as instruments of colonialism in crusade romances. Furthermore, how are these women used to legitimize the power or martial endeavors of the crusaders? In many popular crusade romances, women are often used as tools of conversion, and thus, colonialism. In most romances of the courtly love tradition, women inspire knights to achieve greatness. In crusade romance, Christian damsels may have a different role. The Christian women are often instrumental in converting entire nations by converting their Saracen husbands[2] or, conversely, Saracen princesses are themselves converted to Christianity to marry their chosen

---

[2] A variation of this trope is Isumbras's wife, who is abducted by the Sultan. Once the Sultan is dead and she reunites with her Christian husband, they and their sons embark on a mass conversion of the Saracens together.

knightly Christian lovers. Both types of female characters legitimize the religious violence by perpetuating the often quoted "Christians are right, pagans are wrong" mentality made famous by the *Roland* epic.

Finally, I ask what it means to convert from one identity to another: how does a Saracen (such as Thomas Malory's Palomides) join the Christian community? These popular Middle English romances often establish Englishness and Christianity in opposition to Otherness. Yet, conversions—the process of bringing a pagan into the Christian fold—do not always seem to be entirely effective in terms of accepting a new member into the community. There are some Saracens who are deemed "desirable" converts (and who are portrayed as virtually indistinguishable in appearance and demeanor from their Western counterparts) such as Firumbras and Palomides. But how accepted are they, really? Saracen princesses like Josian and Floripas are usually solitary converts, and often behave in ways that a Christian audience would consider suspect or even treacherous. Even Palomides, widely lauded by scholars as one of Malory's most nuanced and complex characters, cannot escape racial and gendered stereotypes of the Saracen—and as soon as he is baptized, he mostly disappears from the narrative and is only occasionally seen on the fringes of the Arthurian court and tournaments. This seems to suggest that there is an underlying anxiety in Middle English romance about including the Other in the Christian community.

Temporal and Textual Scope

This dissertation focuses specifically on romances in Middle English, except for one Latin romance, *The Rise of Gawain, Nephew of Arthur*. I included *The Rise of Gawain* because it was important to establish a tradition of Eastern influences on Arthurian romance in my third chapter, and this text is considered a part of the Matter of Britain. Middle English

Arthuriana is usually more concerned with British politics and culture, and many times crusading references are relegated to the conclusions of romances to inform audiences of the fates of the knights after the tale is done. In this way, the romances provide appropriate deaths for honorable knights who have completed their domestic duties and are then allowed to chase martyrdom in the crusades. Additionally, because the Arthurian canon has so little contact with the Middle East or crusading, I could not ignore a romance that is partially set in Rome and the Middle East. By the same token, the lack of Saracens in Arthurian romance also helped highlight Malory's Palomides as a fascinating character, because he is both non-English and non-Christian in this very insular world.

The temporal scope of this project centers mainly on texts in the fourteenth and fifteenth centuries. With few exceptions, most of the texts I chose to work with are dated somewhere between 1300 and the mid-1400s. It seemed prudent to keep the scope of this project limited to less than two full centuries, as many of the crusade romances were written during this period. Historically, the fourteenth and fifteenth centuries may be characterized as a time of great change and upheaval: the major crusades were over; the Black Plague ravaged the population from 1348 onwards, prompting the rise of a new middle class; Richard II was deposed in 1399 and replaced by his cousin, Bolingbroke, who became Henry IV; some of the greatest writers of Middle English canon, including Chaucer, Langland, and Gower, were producing their masterpieces; the Hundred Years War between England and France spanned over half of both centuries; and from 1455 to 1485, England was in civil turmoil as the houses of Lancaster and York fought over the English crown. It comes as no surprise that attention turned to identity—who or what were the English people? Moreover, who did they *want* to be? I believe a partial answer to those questions can be found in popular Middle English romances.

The focal text of chapter one is *Richard Coer de Lion* (version A, c. 1450) which exists in two different versions, the A-text and the abbreviated B-text. Dating this romance is a little more difficult because it exists as early as 1330 in the Auchinleck MS (B-text). However, I chose the A-text drawn from the later Gonville and Caius College MS because it was longer and contained some interesting scenes that the B-text does not. The A-text has more cannibalism and contains a reimagining of Plantagenet family folklore in the story of Richard's demon mother. Overall, I found it the more thought-provoking of the two versions, and far more relevant to my purposes than the abbreviated B-text.

My second chapter focuses on three texts which are all firmly fourteenth century, *Firumbras* (c. 1375-1400), *Bevis of Hampton* (c. 1330), and *The King of Tars* (c. 1330). This chapter examines Christian damsels and Saracen princesses, and because there is such a strong tradition of these women in Middle English crusade texts, narrowing my selection down to three was difficult. As for the texts I did include in the second chapter, I chose *Firumbras* and *Bevis of Hampton* because each romance has a spirited and highly intelligent Saracen princess as the heroine. Both heroines exhibit behaviors of the convertible Saracen princess in their willingness to be baptized, their speech patterns, their devotion to their lovers, and both must undergo personal identity change from violent and active Saracen princesses to becoming good Christian women and wives. For my Christian damsel, I chose the unnamed princess from *The King of Tars*, who is a surprising character. She blends hagiographical elements with cool, calculating intelligence to infiltrate and convert an enemy court from within. All three female characters from these romances are far from shy and retiring. They are bright, interesting, and intelligent characters and much of this chapter focuses on how they get what they want.

The latest text I use is the focal text of chapter three: Malory's *Morte Darthur* (finished in 1471 and printed by Caxton in 1485), which pushes close to the line between the English medieval and Early Modern eras. I chose this text because Malory writes the Saracen knight Palomides in an unprecedentedly complex, psychologically nuanced way in "The Book of Tristram." Accompanying this major text are the Latin romance *The Rise of Gawain* (discussed above), and two shorter Arthurian romances *Sir Degrevant* and *Perceval of Galles*. As mentioned before, the Arthurian tradition is insular and concerned more with domestic politics and strife and less with religious crusade and Saracens, but I wanted to show the ways that Arthurian canon does engage, however briefly, with crusade conflict.

In the end, I chose depth over breadth, and so there are several texts I did not or was unable include in this project. For example, *Guy of Warwick*, *The Alliterative Morte*, the Constance tradition, and *Floris and Blancheflour*. An in-depth treatment of the Constance tradition, which includes *Emaré* and Chaucer's The Man of Law's Tale, could well have been a chapter unto itself and did not make it into my project because of time constraints. *Floris and Blancheflour* was not included in chapter two because although the characters are a Saracen prince and a Christian damsel, and the romance is set in the Middle East, the focus of the romance fell outside of my thematic scope: it is more about gender, coming of age, and love rather than religious or political strife. My future work will hopefully give these texts the attention they deserve. For example, an expansion of my focus to include the relationship between Saracens and giants would certainly include *The Alliterative Morte* and *Guy of*

Warwick, and I could include Guy's wife Felice in a wider discussion of accomplished female Christian characters.

Terminology

Medieval studies is an interdisciplinary field, and consequently I have drawn research and ideas from various fields of study to provide a well-rounded analysis of my chosen texts. Throughout this project, I use several terms connected to the various studies of literature, folklore, and postcolonial theory: romance, foodways, liminality, and Saracen. Since these terms may be used differently by different scholars, or have evolved in meaning, I will lay out how I am using them to prevent any confusion.

Romance. Romance is a notoriously difficult genre to define. We can, perhaps, agree with Nicola McDonald that romances were and still are popularly consumed judging by the number of surviving Middle English romances, but that alone is not enough to define the genre (1). Over the past few decades, scholars have worked to compile a criterion for romance, with limited success. John Finlayson, in his famous essay "Definitions of Middle English Romance," perfectly encapsulates the difficulty of defining romance:

> There exists in Middle English a large body of narrative poems, dealing in varied ways with a considerable range of subjects, which literary historians and their dependent critics have agreed to call *romance*. One of the greatest difficulties facing the student of Middle English narrative poetry lies in the ambiguity, or even vagueness, of this designation. By almost common consent, all narratives dealing with aristocratic *personae* and involving combat and/or love are called *romances*, if written after 1100. (429, italics in original)

Clearly, scholars have their work cut out for them. Because romance involves so many different subjects and takes different forms, one scholar's idea of romance might be very different from another's. For instance, Finlayson says "poems" but where does that leave prose romances like Thomas Malory's *Morte Darthur*? Perhaps Yin Liu describes romance best in "Middle English Romance as Prototype Genre." Liu uses cognitive linguistics to argue that romances are prototypal, that is, "not defined by its boundary but by its best examples (its prototypes)" (338). Simply put, even if we do not have a hard and fast definition of romance, we do have a set list of texts that scholars generally agree are romances, albeit of varying degrees of quality. We can take a text and measure it against the romances we know and evaluate it in terms of its components. For example, I chose to examine the *Richard Coer de Lion* A-text over the B-text, because the more sensational A-text better fit with my understanding and expectations of romance whereas the B-text reads more like an epic than a romance. Perhaps this is not a satisfying checklist definition of romance but, as Liu notes, it is a usably flexible one (338). In the end, we know a romance when we see it.

For my purposes, the best way to think of a definition of romance is to look at the texts structurally and thematically. Starting with Finlayson's definition above, I agree with his assessment that romances are about the aristocratic classes and may involve combat (either personal or in war) or love interests. Romances are concerned with a wide array of issues and may be broken down even further in terms of sub-genres which may have their own aims (Arthurian romances, crusade romances, and so on). Gail Ashton argues that,

> Romance is a story of origins—not simply a matter of birthright (although we all recognize the archetypal changeling motif) but a consideration of our place in the wider world with its myths, narratives of history, unstable constructions of class, ethnicity and nationhood, and the impulses and effects of colonization ... Here everyday life is distorted and identities are tried on, tested. This is where the real with all its anxieties and social codes is reconfigured. (1-2)

In other words, a fundamental concern of romance is identity—finding, building, maintaining, challenging, accepting, or rejecting identity on a personal or community level. Ashton also believes that romances are liminal and utopic; that is, they often exist in the twilight zones of reality and history and imagine an ideal world (2). W. R. J. Barron thinks along similar lines in his book, *English Medieval Romance*: "At the heart of the romance mode in all its manifestations certain values remain constant. From ancient Greece to our own age, the search for the ideal has constantly been concerned with the same essential experiences: love, honour, valour, fear, self-knowledge" (4). This is helpful in figuring out a definition of romance, because the romance often does reflect an idyllic, highly stylized image of the world where knights are chivalrous, ladies are beautiful, and magic and the supernatural are real. Romances are inherently liminal, rarely set in any definitive place or time in our world.

Recently, there has been a resurgence in studies of Middle English romance because although the French romance tradition is generally well regarded, English romances have not always enjoyed such respect. This attitude has been changing. McDonald's "A Polemical Introduction" to *Pulp Fictions of Medieval England* outlines the long history of English romance being dismissed for a variety of reasons, including that it is dangerous to the moral and social order (3), and that it serves as a kind of opiate of the masses, which has long been a damning critique of popular culture (10). Nevertheless, McDonald writes, "popular romance provides us with a unique opportunity to explore the complex workings of the medieval imaginary and the world outside the text that feeds and supports it" (1). Essentially, by ignoring the value of English romance because it was popular culture, scholars are missing out on an opportunity to see what drives the medieval imagination. My project, in part, seeks to be a part of this ongoing conversation. Popular culture is usually a good way to see what ideas, hopes, and fears a community or even a nation is wrestling with at that given moment in time.

In sum, when I discuss romance, I mean a popular narrative, whether prose or verse, that contains at least a majority of the following criteria: an aristocratic personage who goes on adventures; engages in some form of physical or psychological violence that is either personal, in a tournament, or in war; acquires a love interest which may either be peripheral to the story or a major driving influence of it; and there are elements of the supernatural (optional, but may include faeries, magic, giants, angels, or demons). The narrative is also atemporal, meaning that it exists outside of any identifiable time. In more specific terms of a crusade romance, I mean all the above, with the addition that the romance is at least partially set in the Middle East or a Christian-Muslim conflict zone (such as *Sir Degrevant*). This narrative may also include fictionalized retellings of actual history, such as *Richard Coer de Lion*. Finally, the crusade romance places emphasis on Christian-Saracen conflict and/or conversion of Saracens to Christianity. This definition is specific enough to apply to a wide range of texts, and to an equally wide range of male and female characters. Under this definition, a knight could be a romance hero and so could a lady like Josian or the princess of Tars.

Foodways. Foodways is a term often used in folklore and food studies. Simply defined, foodways are "the traditional customs or habits of a group of people concerning food and eating" (*OED*). In her essay "Culinary Tourism: A Folkloristic Perspective on Eating and Otherness," Lucy M Long writes that,

> 'foodways' suggests that food is a network of activities and systems—physical, social (communicative), cultural, economic, spiritual, and aesthetic .... As such, food touches every aspect of our lives. Participation in this multifaceted universe involves the procurement and/or the production of raw materials; the preparation of those materials into food; the preservation of foods; the planning of menus and meal systems; the presentation of dishes; the performance of eating styles or techniques; the system of food habits, food ethos, and aesthetics; as well as the actual consumption of food. (23).

Food is intimately connected to personal and culinary identity and, moreover, we are defined by what we do not eat as much as by what we do eat, what we do or do not find palatable. Because foodways are so entrenched in culture, deviations from foodways can be significant. In general, foodways can be summed up by the pithy adage "we are what we eat," but folklorist Millie Rahn wonders if scholars are thinking of foodways backwards and suggests considering if perhaps "we eat what we are" (30). She goes on to write that food expresses our traditions, beliefs, and histories on personal, familial, and community levels. We recreate dishes that are important to us, eat certain foods as part of religious ceremonies or holiday celebrations, and express our ethics and values through our acquisition or growing of it (32).

In other words, at the heart of foodways are ideas of personal and cultural identity, traditions and histories, nationalism, ethics, and religion. This term is of especial importance to my examination of *Richard Coer de Lion* in Chapter One. Although foodways are ever-present in the romance, I pay close attention to the way the text blends a history of crusade famine and deprivation with Richard's fictionalized cannibalism of his Saracen captives.

Liminality. Liminality is a concept often used in postcolonial theory to indicate a state of in-betweenness, thresholds, or gaps in terms of physical location, experience, or identity. In his book *The Location of Culture*, Homi Bhabha uses Renée Green's analysis of her own architectural art to discuss liminality. He examines the function of the stairwell as a liminal space that connects rooms in the building: "The stairwell as liminal space, in-between the designations of identity, becomes the process of symbolic interaction, the connective tissue that constructs the difference between upper and lower, black and white. The hither and thither of the stairwell, the temporal movement and passage it allows, prevents identities at either end of it from settling into primordial polarities" (5). The idea of liminal space being "connective tissue" is an interesting one, because it allows one to vacillate between here and there. Palomides, for example, is liminal throughout most of his story arc in Malory's *Morte Darthur*, because he is always on his way to baptism: he is Saracen by birth, yet professes Christian faith, while putting baptism off (and the consequent decision to remain fully in one religious space or the other) for most of his narrative. He remains caught in the gray area between ideologies until his baptism.

I also find Bjørn Thomassen's idea of liminality valuable to my purposes. He looks at liminality through the lens of the social sciences and thinks of it not only as a space of transition or in-betweenness (or a borderland between cultures), but also as rites of passage that, "render human lives meaningful and bring us from one place to another. Life and death, day and night, light and dark, girl and woman, novice and expert: liminality emerges in the in-between of a passage ... Whenever previously existing borders or limits are lifted away or dissolve into fundamental doubt, the liminal presents itself with a challenge: how to cope with this uncertainty?" (2). In this way, Thomassen expands the idea of liminality to a vast array of experiences and argues that "such transitions mark us, they stamp our personalities" (4). For my purposes, this wider definition of liminality contains implications for personal *and* national identity. If experience makes us who we are on an individual level, it stands to reason that experience undergone as a community may leave similar marks. Considering that each of the major texts examined in this project grapple with various identities through crusade or the Other, we must consider liminality as a mediator that helps determine what it means to be English, Christian, or a combination of the two. Many of the characters I examine deal with liminality, not just Palomides.

Saracen. The term "Saracen" tends to be amorphous, a detail that has been well marked by scholars. "Saracen" can mean nearly anyone non-Christian in medieval literature. Kathy Cawsey writes that "there is actually a long tradition in medieval literature of equating pagans from the North with Muslims from the East and South. Many scholars have noted the way in which the definition of the word 'Saracen' expanded to include all kinds of non-Christian groups" (384). Similarly, Anna Czarnowus notes that many romances consider Saracens to be a monolithic group of pagans that included anyone who was not Christian: "we must remember that at the time Europe itself was not entirely Christian and it did not uniformly belong to Christian culture" (9). Generally, romances were uninterested in differentiating between various religious sects, so the historically complex politics of Sunni versus Shi'ite branches of Islam would be subsumed into one generic term of Saracen. To be fair, in these romances Christians are considered to be uniform as well—the better to construct the us/them binary. In any case, I use the term "Saracen" to mean the *textual* Muslim character as found in the romances I examine. As Siobhain Bly Calkin notes in *Saracens and the Making of English Identity*, rarely does the textual Saracen reflect the lived experiences, ideologies, or faith of actual medieval Muslims (1). However, the textual Saracens do magnify the inherent racial and religious prejudices of the medieval English romance audience. Leona Cordery writes,

> It was the aristocratic, chivalric class that made up the audience for the literary authors of the day and served as patrons of the arts. Therefore, anyone writing in this period who was financially dependent had to write in keeping with the audience. These interests, among others, focused on the East. First, this was seen as a new, mystical world, with ideas fired by pilgrims and Crusaders and the reports they brought back with them. At the same time the people of the East presented a threat not only militarily, as had been made very clear at the very latest at the Battle of Poitiers, but also spiritually, as the religious enemy that wanted to annihilate Christianity. This is the kind of material we find in the works of the authors at this time. (88)

The East (including the Middle East) was simultaneously a fascination for audiences—romances are peppered with references to silk and samite, representations of extreme wealth, and spices—and a place of conflict, particularly the Holy Land. With all but the first Crusade ending in failure or stalemate, the romances provided aristocratic audiences with a "win" where the fictional English knight-hero manages what the real-life knights and soldiers could not do: conquer or convert the Muslims to Christianity. The textual Saracen is essentially fictional wish-fulfillment: an enemy to defeat; a beautiful and powerful princess to woo; a new convert to the Christian cause. Thus, with respect to those who suffered in what was clearly a traumatic series of conflicts that have reverberated even into contemporary politics and Western prejudices, I try to be specific when I use terms: *Saracen* for the fictional, textual references, and *Muslim* if I am speaking of real-life people or histories.

Methodology: Postcolonial Theory

Although medieval studies in general has had a hesitant relationship with theory—there are difficulties and ethical concerns attached to utilizing certain modern theories on pre-modern societies and texts—I do draw on quite a few critics who are concerned with ideas of race, religion, and (post)colonialism. My study of postcolonial theory and medieval studies starts on the well-trod ground of Edward Said's work, *Orientalism*, which is widely accepted as a groundbreaking work that offers a comprehensive critique of nineteenth-century ideas of colonialism and imperialism. Said argues that orientalism arose as a way for the West to try to exert the power of narrative over the East: "Orientalism can be discussed and analyzed as the corporate institution for dealing with the Orient—dealing with it by making statements about it, authorizing views of it, describing it, teaching it, settling it, ruling over it: in short, Orientalism is a Western style for dominating, restructuring, and having authority over the

Orient" (3). The West constructs and perpetuates an image of the Orient that is not necessarily grounded in either reality or lived experience. The West makes up its mind about how the East should be perceived and ignores the complexity about what it is. Orientalism, in short, says far more about the West and its mindsets and values than it ever does about the East (22). And yet, according to Said, scholars appear to be resistant to the idea that texts—and scholars themselves—are influenced by sociopolitical concerns and hegemony. Intertextuality is acceptable when discussing how one text connects to another in style, ideology, or any other common marker; however, in an academic institution that values objectivity above all else, the idea that authors/texts and scholars could themselves be the product of political and ideological intertextuality (and thus unknowingly apply it to their own work) makes humanist scholars nervous (13).

Said's study provides a framework and a standard starting point for working with postcolonial theory; however, I acknowledge the difficulties arising from the application of a modern theory to the Middle Ages. Said writes about nineteenth-century issues of colonialism and race, and he often references or connects his writing to real world events. While he does discuss Dante's *Inferno*, his analysis has been critiqued as lacking by medievalists who found his application of Orientalism to Dante as unnecessarily reductionist (Lampert-Weissig 14). Clearly, elements of *Orientalism*, more comfortable with a modern scope, need refining in terms of medieval (post)colonialism. After all, for all the warfare that characterized the English Middle Ages, both in local wars between England and its immediate neighbors and in the Crusades, England could only dream about the heights of colonial power it would someday reach.

In addition to the problem of adapting a theory to an era it was not originally meant for, scholars like Catherine Brown have ethical reservations about using a postcolonial lens to interpret the Middle Ages, even if she agrees that there are advantages to using it:

> Colonial and postcolonial theory does indeed help us see important things about the Middle Ages and about the practice of medieval studies. But I don't want to appropriate or apply it. For one thing, the knowledge/power activities of the two disciplines in the world of the living are incommensurable in ethically crucial ways: medievalism will never affect the lives of medieval people as Orientalism has affected and continues to affect the lives of living people. In addition, any theory's creative reach is limited if it is used instrumentally, applied to a medieval body imagined as inert object by a theory-wielding *sujet-supposé-à-savoir*. And if we're taking colonial and postcolonial theory seriously, we should be especially troubled by the modernizing agenda implicit in the *application* of theory, as if theory's task were to bring marginal medievalism up to date and integrate it into the intellectual life of the academic metropolis. Such a gesture rings uncannily with the modernizing mission of colonialism: it reaches down to take up the theoretician's burden, to bring theory to the backward. (550)

Although she talks specifically about medievalism[3] here instead of medieval studies, her reticence about the former can easily be applied to discussions of the latter. The field of medieval studies does have inherent colonial impulses because we are interpreting and viewing the medieval through a modern lens. We run the risk of overwriting the Middle Ages with ideas and terminology that would have been alien to the original time. For instance, contemporary white supremacist groups, like the German Nazis before them, are currently using medieval studies and *deus vult* crusading ideology to argue that the Europe of the Middle Ages was entirely white, an idea which has been soundly discredited by medieval scholars.[4] This misuse of medieval studies only highlights the dangers inherent in

---

[3] "Medievalism" is the study of any post-medieval recreations of the medieval across a broad range of texts (*Lord of the Rings*, the BBC *Merlin*, some of the paintings of the 19th century Pre-Raphaelite Brotherhood, renaissance fairs, the themed attraction *Medieval Times*, etc.) whereas "medieval studies" studies actual medieval texts, history, and society. My dissertation focuses on medieval studies.

[4] For more context on this debate, see "The far right's new fascination with the Middle Ages" from *The Economist*, Paul B. Sturdevant's "Race, Racism, and the Middle Ages: Tearing down the 'Whites Only' Medieval World" from *The Public Medievalist*, J. Clara Chan's "Medievalists, Recoiling from White

approaching medieval texts with a modern mindset. Considering all the possible abuses of theory (especially one that is applied to a time and people long gone and thus unable to speak for themselves), Brown wonders at the appropriateness of using a theory that continues to have a demonstrable impact on entire groups of people in our own time. Orientalist stereotypes and fetishes, proxy wars fought during and after the Cold War, and Western destabilization of the Middle East and East, are all ongoing issues. In contrast, medieval scholars can be lulled into a false sense of security because the medieval period and its inhabitants are unable to speak for themselves or share their experience; all we have are the surviving texts from which we try to reconstruct the Middle Ages. This leads to Brown's second point: that, ironically, in using postcolonial theory to try and understand the Middle Ages (or even to trace back the roots of modern colonialism and imperialism) we risk colonizing the past with our own preconceptions, identity, and culture. If Orientalism ultimately says more about the Western societies that produce it, then by the same token our methods of engaging with the medieval world say more about us today than it probably ever could about them back then.

Nevertheless, scholars are learning to adapt and apply postcolonial theory to the medieval and early modern periods. According to Bruce Holsinger in his essay "Medieval Studies, Postcolonial Studies, and the Genealogies of Critique," the intersection between medieval studies and postcolonial theory is not only inevitable, but natural:

> While recent encounters between postcolonial studies and medieval studies have opened up new lines of inquiry into the nature of premodern forms of colonialism and imperialism, it is worth remembering that, at least in certain areas of our field, scholars have long been engaged in projects that resonate compellingly with the critical impulses of postcolonialism. With little or no help from postcolonial theory,

---

Supremacy, Try to Diversify the Field" from *The Chronicle of Higher Education*, and Gene Demby's "Taking a Magnifying Glass to the Brown Faces in Medieval Art" from *NPR*.

> in other words, more than a few medievalists have addressed the very constellation of critical imperatives now at the center of postcolonial critique, demonstrating what I would call the mutually clarifying capacities of medieval and postcolonial studies. (1200)

Simply put, Holsinger argues that whatever reservations we might have about the applicability of the theory to medieval studies, we cannot avoid it because we are already doing it. Critical works like Norman Daniel's *Islam and the West*, and R.W. Southern's *Western Views of Islam in the Middle Ages*, have been instrumental in turning the conversation to medieval ideas of Otherness. Scholars have been following postcolonial lines of inquiry and examining ideas of empire, nationalism, and identity in medieval texts for decades now. Such things are difficult to miss, particularly in crusade romances. *Richard Coer de Lion, Guy of Warwick, Bevis of Hampton, The King of Tars* and other texts examined in this dissertation can be read as meditations on what it means to be English and/or to be Christian (or Western), and how those identities can be fortified or threatened. Postcolonial theory gives medievalists another theoretical toolkit to use.

Benedict Robinson, in his *Islam and Early Modern English Literature*, furthers the use of postcolonial theory in less-than-ideal time periods: "The presence or absence of empire cannot be the sole condition of relevance of theories that are more concerned with the intellectual and cultural dispositions enabling empire, and with the multiple ways in which nations and communities have imagined and constituted themselves" (12). In other words, one way to consider medieval postcolonialism is to look at the emerging English national and cultural identities that were beginning to coalesce during the latter half of the Middle Ages. Robinson might not be working with specifically medieval literature in his treatise, but the way he applies the theory to early modern romance proves instructive. According to Robinson, the romance genre is concerned with identity and difference: "As the literary form that thinks most intensely about difference, romance evokes characteristically mixed moods: love and war, conversion and crusade, seduction and violence. It does not merely represent difference but attempts to think difference in its widest possible significance" (4). This meditation on difference, on building national identities based on "us" and "them," on setting the stage for later imperial conquests, can be found in medieval works where the representations of Saracens reveal more about the English mind and fantasies than any actual lived experience of a Muslim.

Some scholars have also begun to locate ideas of modern colonialism in the Middle Ages. Lisa Lampert-Weissig does not focus specifically on English literature, but her *Medieval Literature and Postcolonial Studies* is invaluable for understanding the current postcolonial conversations in medieval studies. She believes the groundwork of later empires was laid during the Middle Ages: "the medieval foundations of colonialism and later interpretations of these foundations—that is, both scholarly medieval studies and the popular medievalisms found in all kinds of cultural production—have been essential to the vision of Europe as a progressive and enlightened global centre, a centre that is defined in large part through contrast to non-Europeans" (2). Centuries of crusading in the Middle East and upheavals in the Church all contribute to the formation of European identity. In *Medieval Boundaries: Rethinking Difference in Old French Literature*, Sharon Kinoshita also maintains that studies in medieval postcolonialism consider the medieval period "as the site of the origin, or at least the consolidation, of the emergent ideologies of European colonial expansionism" (1). For Kinoshita, medieval postcolonialism highlights the intricacies of the thirteenth-fifteenth centuries: the Hundred Years War, the conflict between emerging popular vernacular works and the official culture of Latinate works, the uneasy relationship between

Christians and Muslims both in text and in reality, and even the malleable geographic and linguistic boundaries of Europe all constitute a Gordian knot of political, religious, and cultural difference that would set the stage for future colonial endeavors (4-6). Furthermore, In *Empire of Magic*, Geraldine Heng melds the study of English romance with postcolonialism by locating ideas of empire in romances. She examines the way that ideas of empire and colonialism are treated throughout centuries of romance—from ideas of military superiority to ideas of incorporation of the Other via religious conversion (6).

In addition to postcolonial considerations, throughout this project I also am mindful of the methodologies of cultural poetics or new historicism. If one of the pitfalls to using postcolonial theory is the danger of colonizing the past, then perhaps it is a good policy to situate texts in conversation with each other and with the histories, audiences, and cultures that produced them. For instance, a conversation about romance-Richard's desire for pork and subsequent textual cannibalism of Saracens must be understood in terms of the complex medieval foodways and historically documented famines. Understanding the princess of Tars means engaging with hagiography, sexual politics, and cultural fears of miscegenation. Literature does not happen in a vacuum, but is intertwined with politics, religion, and the cultures that produce or are affected by it.

Other Key Criticism

Over the past couple of decades, especially post-9/11, there has been a resurgence in scholarship on medieval representations of Islam in early English texts. Conflict between the Middle East and the West does not exist in a vacuum, and scholars like Suzanne Conklin Akbari and Siobhain Bly Calkin have gone looking for the ways the East and West have interacted in pre-modern texts. Akbari's *Idols in the East* surveys a broad range of texts from encyclopedias and maps to *chansons de geste* and romances to illustrate how the medieval European mind understood the world. This understanding is complicated by the tacit acknowledgement that "the dominant power in the world was not the Christian West but rather the Islamic East, and European awareness of that inferiority played a crucial role in the development of Orientalism" (9). Akbari focuses on both religious and geographical alterity—for medieval Christians, defining what Islam was and where it was located helped Europeans to form and solidify their own identities.

Siobhain Bly Calkin examines representations of the Saracen in the Auchinleck manuscript in her *Saracens and the Making of English Identity*. Her main argument is that while the Saracens in the manuscript in no way depict the actual lived experiences of real Muslims, they reveal clues about the culture that would consume such texts—from the hagiographies to the romances. The Auchinleck manuscript is the product of an emerging English national identity: a moment when the English language began to acquire prestige at the expense of the Anglo-Norman language, when issues of sovereignty made international relationships between England and its neighbors fraught with bloody potential (12). She argues that the representations of the Saracen in the manuscript require "medieval English readers' consideration of what counts as cultural, ethnic, and religious difference, what is to be done about such difference, and how difference and borders between groups are to be negotiated" (7). She dedicates multiple chapters to troubling such boundaries; in her discussion of Saracen knights and women, for example, she highlights the idea that some Saracen characters are presented as attractive candidates for conversion to Christianity, while others are irredeemably Saracen.

Jacqueline de Weever's influential book *Sheba's Daughters* follows the same lines of thinking about convertible Saracens. Although she writes about Saracen women in the French epic tradition, many of her ideas apply equally to the Saracen princesses populating English romances. She considers the implications of race, religion, and gender—specifically the whitened Saracen princesses who are amenable to converting to Christianity. For those characters, Weever argues, nothing is quite as it seems:

> The description of white Saracen women, daughters of black Saracens, seeks to solve the questions of the plot's actions—independence, treason, conversion on the women's part—by producing portraits to facilitate acceptance by the listening audience. These portraits, however, mask deep fears and prohibitions current during the period of their construction. The portrait thus becomes a multivalent instrument of chaos, upsetting aesthetic, religious, and psychological traditions as it aims at inclusion of persons generally thought of as undesirable and dangerous to the culture of the medieval Latin West. (xvi)

In other words, the romance presents the Saracen princess in a way that seems, on the surface, to be non-threatening. A closer examination reveals the paradox and the anxieties about the Other that she embodies: she is Other but looks like the Self; she is treacherous and betrays her family and people but is loyal to her Christian lover; she is a Saracen who converts to Christianity, but her motives are always suspect. The Saracen princess is at once an engaging heroine and the bogeyman, an outsider able to integrate into a new community which she already physically resembles. In the end, the audience is left wondering, then how do we really know who is us and who is them? Religious, racial, and national identities are all destabilized.

In a work that melds medieval romance with modern sheikh romance novels, Amy Burge's *Representing Difference in the Medieval and Modern Orientalist Romance* takes a comparative look at the ways the East is represented in the popular imaginations of Western audiences both in the medieval era and our post-9/11 world. On the surface, the choice of texts may seem incongruous, but Burge argues, "given the provocative connections between postcolonial studies and medievalism, medieval and modern Orientalist romance, positioned across the axis of medieval and modern, East and West, Saracen and Christian, is particularly well placed for comparative analysis" (15). Her focus on both medieval and contemporary romances lends even more credibility to the argument that postcolonial studies should be incorporated with medieval studies. If the groundwork for future empire and ideas of the East began to germinate in the Middle Ages, as argued above, a comparative study of romance then and now indicates the presence of enduring orientalist thoughts and stereotypes.

While I appreciate the difficulties and ethics of applying postcolonial theory to medieval texts, I also fall into the camp that this branch of theory and the field of medieval studies are inextricably intertwined and even complementary. I find myself in the critical company of Akbari, Calkin, and Heng, because my major focus is on the way religion, race, and nationalism inform medieval English identity, or at least, the fictional ideal identity as set out in the various Middle English romances I examine.

Dissertation Outline

Chapter one examines *Richard Coer de Lion*, and the varying images of the Saracens and the East throughout the romance. The text is focused on building and subverting a national English identity in a myriad of ways: through the (re)imagining of Richard as a quintessential English king and hero; by placing the English in opposition to both the French and Saracens in the text; through foodways; and through Richard's interaction with various Saracens, including a highly fictionalized Saladin. Furthermore, the romance legitimizes Richard's crusading in the Holy Land by rewriting his mother, the French Eleanor of Aquitaine, as Cassodorien, the demon princess of Antioch. Moreover, once Richard gets to the Middle East, he engages in two episodes of cannibalism where he eats captive Saracens. Finally, I examine a literal image of a Saracen in the episode of the Marble King. Throughout the romance, Saracens (including Saladin) are used in a variety of ways to contrast with Richard and the English. In this romance, identity is an amorphous, complicated, ever changing idea. The hero of the story is a king of dubious, possibly demonic, parentage which troubles the boundaries of his constructed identity—and that of the English by association.

Chapter two focuses on female characters and conversion. The Saracen princesses Floripas of *Firumbras* and Josian of *Bevis of Hampton* are examined alongside the nameless Christian princess in *The King of Tars*. In this chapter, I examine the way women in the text function as tools of religious colonialism through conversion, and as male power fantasies. The Saracen princesses highlight the ways that Christian male power is artificial and requires the assent of women, because part of the conversion process for the irrepressible Saracen princess is to learn to put aside her own identity to conform to Christian standards of sedate, passive good European womanhood. In contrast, the princess of Tars uses her passivity to lull her Saracen husband into a false sense of security while she waits for the right moment to prove the validity of her religion over his—a chance which arrives with the birth of the lump of flesh. Ultimately the conversions of, or facilitated by, these women legitimize crusade endeavors by upholding the idea that only Christianity is true, right, and legitimate.

Chapter three considers Thomas Malory's liminal Saracen knight, Palomides, as a subject of colonization via conversion and as an example for the difficulties inherent in maintaining various identities of knight, lover, and Saracen/Christian. As a Saracen knight who desperately wants acceptance into the Christian Arthurian community, Palomides is always on his way to baptism; however, unlike many Saracen knights who decide to convert to Christianity, Palomides vows to fight seven battles on Christ's behalf before he will consent to baptism. Malory's version of Palomides in the *Morte Darthur* is easily one of the most nuanced and complex Saracen characters in medieval English romance: he is one of the best knights in the Arthurian world but insecure and emotionally turbulent; the unrequited lover of Isode; the rival/friend of Tristram; and a Saracen who believes in the Christian god.

Throughout all the chapters are discussions of liminality and how representations of Saracens both trouble and help define Christian and/or English identity. This project also considers how the various romances seek to solve the perceived problem of the East, through legitimized violence or through converting the Other to Christianity and making them part of the Self—a process which is heavily burdened with anxieties about miscegenation and contamination of the community. Furthermore, I consider the way that the texts reimagine the failed or stalemated crusades and rewrite them as Western victories.

Chapter 1: *Richard Coer de Lion* and The Construction of English Identity

In this chapter, I will discuss the romance of *Richard Coer de Lion* in terms of identity and nation-building: the erasure of Richard's historical Frenchness through language and lineage; the foodways which demarcate religions; Richard's cannibalism of Saracens; and the religious conversion of a city after Richard defeats the stone image of their king. First, the poet makes it very clear that this is an English romance—written in the English language for the English people about an English king. The poet choosing English as the language of transmission effectively begins the erasure of the historical Richard's own complex Anglo-Norman identity and rewrites Richard as a quintessential champion of the English. The erasure continues with the inclusion of Cassodorien, the demon princess of Antioch, who both fulfills Plantagenet family folklore and replaces the French Eleanor of Aquitaine with a reimagined Melusine-character. In the romance, historical Richard's Frenchness is rewritten as ambiguously Byzantine and demonic. Of course, because the romance constantly uses food as a motif, a discussion of identity must include foodways; after all, we are what we eat. Richard's desire for pork in the Middle East leads to two episodes of cannibalism, wherein he devours his Saracen enemies, further complicating his demonic nature, even as the humanity of the Saracens is questioned. Finally, as the romance winds its way to a conclusion, the poet begins to redeem Richard's demonic nature when he converts a city of Saracens to Christianity after he defeats a stone image of a Saracen king. The episode highlights not only Richard's divine favor, but also the inefficacy of Saracen gods and leadership.

In the romance, the English identity needs opposition for contrast, and thus is best defined against the threats posed by the Middle East and the Saracens in the text. Although it is tempting to present the English and Saracen identities as separate and even opposites, the romance deviously troubles the boundaries that initially seem black and white. For instance, Richard's mother is a demon princess of Antioch, a woman from the Latin East where the contact zones between Christians and Saracens would have been close even in the predominantly Christian city. Her ethnicity seems to be in question, particularly as the text keeps referring to Richard as a devil. Complicating matters of identity further, Richard is often placed in opposition to the French. Alan Ambrisco and Nicola McDonald have both noted this; McDonald argues, "English identity is constructed not simply in opposition to the racially marked infidel, but also against the treachery of the French" (129). The replacement of the historical Richard's mother Eleanor of Aquitaine with romance-Richard's demon mother helps erase Richard's historical French identity. Henry II's own historical Frenchness as the former Duke of Anjou is never mentioned at all in the romance, which opens in England and sees the king meeting Cassodorien and her father at Westminster (*RCL* 153). The adjustment of Richard's lineage on both sides has the benefit of alienating his character from the French, while building ties with the Middle East.

Furthermore, both in history and romance, Richard's relationship with the French king Philip Augustus II is tempestuous. In the romance, the French king continually tries to undermine Richard, and Richard has no qualms battling and killing the French armies if he believes them cowards or if they harass English troops and holdings (1948-50). The final parting between the two kings in the text is tense: Philip wants Richard to win and give him Jerusalem: "Jerusalem, that ryche cytée, / Though thou it wynne it schal be myn" (5856-7), a proposition to which Richard retorts,

> By God, quod Richard, and Seynt Austyn,
> And as God doo my soule boote,

> Off my wynnyng half a foote
> Thou ne schalt have off no lande,
> I doo thè wel to undyrstande!
> And, yiff thou wylt have it, he sayde then,
> Goo, and gete it with thy men! (5858-64).

The poet paints the French King (and by extension, the French as a whole) as unreasonable and lazy. Philip's expectation that Richard will simply win and hand over one of the wealthiest cities in the Middle East is clearly outrageous, and Richard tells Philip that if he wants Jerusalem so badly, then he can do the work of capturing it himself because Richard will not give over even a half a foot of land he has rightfully won in battle. Shortly after this exchange, Philip has had enough of both crusading and Richard and decides to return to France, claiming ailment as his cause, even getting one of his physicians to verify his claim (5872) even though the previous line says that Philip was sick for ire. Richard, who by this point has suffered illness and hardship himself, is appalled at the French king's excuse:

> Kyng Richard on hym gan crye,
> And sayd, he dede gret velonye
> To wende home for maladye
> Out of the londe off Surrye,
> Tyl done were Godes servyse,
> For lyff or deth, in ony wyse.
> The kyng of Fraunce wolde hym nought here,
> But departyd in this manere;
> And aftyr that partyng, forsothe,
> Ever yitt they were wrothe. (5879-88)

The French king and his retinue withdraw from the field and the romance, and the poet mentions that their relationship—fraught during the best of times—never recovered. Once more, the poet maintains Richard's dedication to the cause, his bravery, and his willingness to suffer and die for God's work as a standard that all others in the text inevitably fall short of achieving.

In terms of logistics, *Richard Coer de Lion* (*RCL*) is a romance that survives in seven medieval manuscripts and two early modern editions, suggesting that it was a popular tale in its time. It was based on a lost Anglo-Norman twelfth-century romance, but the earliest surviving text is in the Auchinleck MS, compiled sometime during the 1330s (Burnley and Wiggins). There are indications that *RCL*'s popularity was not without controversy, because there are two versions of the romance, the A and B texts. Of the seven manuscripts that contain the romance, two manuscripts contain a longer version of *RCL*, called the A texts. The differences between the versions are important not just in terms of content but also of genre. The A texts contain more romance tropes and episodes, including the demon mother, the eating of the lion's heart, and a second episode of cannibalism. The A text begins with the legend of Richard's demon mother and the episode wherein Richard disguises himself and defeats his best knights in a tournament. However, the other five manuscripts, including the Auchinleck, contain the B text. The B texts lack the sensational episodes, which indicates to Leila Naruko that the salacious details of the A text were not palatable enough for inclusion into B texts (Naruko "Richard Coer de Lion"). The B text does not have such extraneous detail; instead the B text begins with Richard preparing for crusade. According to John Finlayson, "the A version clearly is an expansion of the B, or original, version, which sways the tenor of the Richard story quite firmly into the ethos of the romance of adventure … In essence the B version is not a romance of adventure but an historical epic, with more historical veracity than any of the O.F. *chansons de geste*" (160-61). The A text is clearly more focused on sensationalism and on building national identity, albeit through unconventional means (cannibalism, demon mother).

Interestingly, dating the manuscripts does not necessarily indicate the version of the text. The early fourteenth-century Auchinleck MS contains a B text of *RCL*, whereas A texts in the Gonville and Caius College MS and the London MS Additional 31042 were both compiled later, at approximately the same time during the early to mid-fifteenth century. One of the earliest editions of *RCL*, published by Wynkyn de Worde in 1509, used the A text (*Database of Middle English Romance*). A further problem arises when we consider the fragmentary nature of some of the manuscripts. The most complete versions of the tale are over 7000 lines, yet some versions have decidedly fewer, including: Auchinleck (heavily fragmented, 1500 lines), London MS Harley (2275 lines), and Duke of Beaufort MS (most of this *RCL* is missing).

For the purposes of this work, I am using Henry Weber's 1810 edition of the A text of *RCL*, found in the second volume of his three-volume work, *Metrical Romances of the Thirteenth, Fourteenth, and Fifteenth Centuries*. Weber uses the early fifteenth-century Gonville and Caius College MS as the source of his edition because he considers it "the most perfect copy" of the tale in current existence, even if it does lack several leaves (xlviii). Although the thirteenth-century Auchinleck MS is the earliest surviving version of the romance, Weber prefers the Gonville and Caius College MS because he believes it is the most complete surviving copy of the romance: "the Auchinleck fragment has much of the air of a mere abridgment" (xlvii).[5] As a point of interest, the Gonville and Caius College MS contains only three works. *Richard Coer de Lion* is framed by the shorter romances *Athelston* and *Sir Isumbras*. *Athelston* is a romance about an English king and his struggle with court

---

[5] Finlayson would disagree with this assessment. Because the *RCL* in the Auchinleck predates the other manuscripts, "it is taken to represent the version closest to the original English version of a lost Anglo-Norman work" (161). Although, without the original Anglo-Norman work itself, it seems an unsupportable position.

intrigue. The romance focuses on ideas of treason and English law. The other text, *Sir Isumbras*, is a popular romance which contains elements of pilgrimage and holy war as the titular hero battles against Saracens for the sake of his soul, wife, and family. Taken together, this manuscript grapples with English nationalism in court, in law, in war, and in religion.

English Language and Nationalism

RCL is a multilayered meditation on Englishness (of which the English language itself is a tool) and so the author's care in pointing out that this is a work in English makes sense. The romance presents language as intrinsic to national identity. *RCL* is ostensibly a romance of a famous English king, written in English, for the English people. Throughout the high Middle Ages in England, the push for English was a controversial one in a culture where Latin and Anglo-Norman were the language of the courts, scholars, and aristocracy respectively, while English was the language of the lower and emerging middle and merchant classes. One need but recall the Lollard heresy in the late fourteenth century to understand the subversive power of texts (namely the Bible) made available to a wider audience in a more accessible common language.

In his essay "The Politics of Middle English Writing," Nicholas Watson argues, "Middle English writing was and went on being much preoccupied with its own legitimacy and status, while the use of written English, both in England itself and Scotland, was highly politically charged throughout the period" (331). The rise of English had further political implications in the way it could potentially unite a people under one language. The young Henry V followed this line of thinking when, as a prince, he commissioned works in English from Hoccleve and Lydgate. Chaucer, Langland, and Gower also used English politically in their own writings. Langland's *Piers Plowman* was written during a time of unrest that culminated in the 1381 Peasant's Revolt, and Gower's *Confessio Amantis* "makes its own use of social complaint and satire and addresses its elite audience from the perspective not of the crown or nobility but that of the 'commons,' offering advice to church and crown with a freedom that fifteenth-century literature was not encouraged to emulate" (Watson 349). Clearly, a shared language is a double-edged sword: on the one hand, a common language can draw together a nation through mutual or widespread understanding. On the other hand, it can also facilitate social and political unrest when a group, such as "the commons," acquires the literacy and knowledge needed to resist a status quo they find oppressive or disagreeable.

RCL's intention is nation-building when it promises to tell inspiring stories in the English language of the doughty knights of England to anyone who desires to listen (26-28). However, identity-construction does not happen in a vacuum. Defining what it means to be English means highlighting what it means to be Other than English. Suzanne Conklin Akbari, like Ambrisco, notes that the English identity is often built in opposition to the other cultural groups in the romance, particularly, but not limited to, the French:

> [T]he conflict of the French and the English is one of a series of encounters that result in the definition of English national identity and the recognition of its superiority. This is not to deny that the French identity of the historical Richard I is suppressed in the romance's construction of a purely English kind, but to assert that English identity is constructed in the romance in a dynamic way, through the repeated encounter with a series of other nations, each of which differs from that of the English and comes to acknowledge its own inferiority. (205)

Indeed, the romance is only partly constructed in opposition to the French, since it also includes Greece and the Middle East. The poet situates Richard among the great romance figures of the time—Arthur and Gawain for the English, Roland and Charlemagne for the French, and even the classical Greek figures of Achilles and Hector, effectively covering the

English, French, and Latin East/Middle Eastern regions and nationalities that will be important throughout the romance (*RCL* 10-19).

With the other Worthies already laid out in the opening lines, the poet then goes on to make very clear the fact that this romance is English. Richard's historical allegiances and identity aside, and while he might be placed and remembered among the greats of romance and *chansons de geste*, Richard represents the English in *RCL*, not the French. Yet, the poet claims that the romance is a translation from a French source:

> In Frensshe bookys this rym is wrought,
> Lewede menne knowe it nought;
> Lewede menne cunne French non;
> Among an hondryd unnethis on;
> And nevertheles, with glad chere,   25
> Fele off hym that wolde here,
> Noble justis, I undyrstonde,
> Of doughty knyghtes off Yngelonde. (21-28)

Taken at face value, the poet is presenting the audience with a helpful English translation of a French work, but a closer look at the passage reveals a contradictory tone of cynicism. The motivation for this translation is revealed by the poet's claim that unlearned men do not know the original French text and because of the language barrier, could not read or understand it even if they did. Thus, to reach an English audience with a tale about one of their own kings, the poet takes it upon himself to provide the masses with a comprehensible translation of the original text in the English language since the target audience cannot manage French anymore. The statistic that only one in a hundred men knows enough French to muddle their way through the original text is a damning way to reinforce the preceding two lines. Furthermore, despite an allusion to cheerfulness, line 25 does not dispel the poet's ruefulness regarding the language skills of his audience—in fact, the word "nevertheles" functions as a linguistic dismissal that highlights his dim view of his English audience's lack of proficiency in French, a dismissal that is reinforced in subsequent lines where he says, "*Par foie*, now I woll yow rede / Off a kyng, doughty in dede" (29-30). The laconic "*par foie*" ("by faith") reads as one last cynical lament of his audience's lack of French before he continues to read to his audience in English. The insistence on English as the mode of storytelling is but the first way the poet erases the historical Richard's Frenchness and rebuilds him as the quintessential English hero. There was still the matter of Richard's French heritage to contend with, so the poet reimagines Plantagenet family folklore in order to cut ties with France and build new ones in the Latin East.

Cassodorien, Demon Princess of Antioch

In *RCL*, Richard's historical Frenchness is erased and replaced through his literary mother, Cassodorien, a gorgeous and fabulously wealthy princess of Antioch (*RCL* 64). Although she occupies a small portion of the overall romance and is never mentioned after her flying escape, Cassodorien is more than just an example of a fantastical element of romance or a re-imagining of Richard's family legends. She is a key to understanding the rest of the text, and even legitimizes Richard's later crusading endeavors more than Eleanor of Aquitaine could have. Not only is Cassodorien of ostensibly Middle Eastern origin—which calls into question Richard's own ethnicity—but she also appears to be a demon. She is first introduced aboard a ship of outrageous wealth and is taken back to England to wed the young King Henry (73-76). After she passes out during the wedding ceremony, Cassodorien starts slipping out of church right before the Mass and does so unhindered for fifteen years. However, her inability to remain for the entire Mass does not go unnoticed, and when the king and his men eventually force her to remain she flies out of the church with her daughter and is never seen again (73-240).

The romance uses a repurposed version of an actual Plantagenet family legend that Richard himself liked to retell in company. In his book, *The Demon's Brood: A History of the Plantagenet Dynasty*, Desmond Seward examines the legend and the Plantagenets, who allegedly descend from a demon ancestor named Melusine:

> According to Gerald of Wales[6], the tale of Melusine was frequently told by King Richard, who said that with such an ancestor it was not surprising that he and his brothers quarreled. 'We come from the Devil and we'll end by going to the Devil,' joked the Lionheart. What might be termed diabolical genes were part of the family inheritance. (Seward xviii).

Seward briefly summarizes Gerald of Wales's tale of the Plantagenet's demon ancestor: the father or grandfather of the Black Fulk (Richard's own several-times great grandfather) encountered a woman named Melusine while he was out hunting. She possessed an unearthly beauty, and even though he met her in the middle of a forest, he decided to marry her immediately. Melusine bore him four children, but refused to attend church except rarely, and even then, she slipped out early in the service. When the king and his court tried to make her stay, she tucked two of her children under her arms and flew out of the church, never to been seen again (Seward xvii). Whether a truth of any kind exists in this story, as Sewell notes above, Richard was enchanted by it. Certainly, even a cursory examination of the dynasty reveals that their allegedly supernatural bloodline aside, they fought and often lost to their personal demons as often as they fought each other. In *Richard Coer de Lion*, the tale of Melusine[7] is repurposed. Instead of a shadowy ancestor blurred by at least half a dozen generations, Richard's actual mother Eleanor of Aquitaine is replaced by Cassodorien, the

---

[6] According to the *Encyclopaedia Britannica*, Gerald of Wales (1146-1223), was both a noted historian and archdeacon of Brecknock. He attended university in Paris, and he was a courtier of both Henry II and Richard I.

[7] There is a French prose romance by Jean d'Arras called *Melusine: or, The Noble History of Lusignan*, dated from 1393. Donald Maddox and Sara Sturm-Maddox note that, "*Melusine*, as the late fourteenth-century reader might well have recognized, is a name associated in myth and folklore with a supernatural female creature" (1). Clearly, Melusine was a supernatural figure of some popularity to be included in centuries-long folklore.

beautiful and mysterious princess of Antioch. As noted above, Cassodorien's story is much the same as Melusine's—the aversion to the Mass, the queen's habit of slipping out before it begins, and the dramatic flying escape with her children are all events retold in *RCL*. Notably, Cassodorien initially snatches up both her daughter, Topyas, and John, but drops and abandons John (229-34). She does not try to abduct the teenaged Richard.

This part of the romance is particularly interesting not only for the bizarre events it contains, but also for what it does not. Along with Richard's Frenchness, the romance also erases the historical Richard's brothers William, Henry the Young King, and Geoffrey from the narrative, likely to save time in recounting the overall story without the digressions of the family strife. Unlike reality, in the romance the only person between Richard and the crown is his father. The teenaged Richard is quickly named Henry's heir:

> For her love, that was servyd so,
> Wolde [Henry] never aftyr com ther, ne go.
> He let ordeyne, after hys endynge,
> His sone Rychard to be kyng. (236-40)

It is also notable that King Henry dies of a broken heart soon after Cassodorien's abandonment, instead of exhausted old age after decades of trying to control his unruly sons and equally tempestuous wife, Eleanor of Aquitaine. Like the legendary king Arthur, romance Richard ascends the throne at the age of fifteen and immediately turns his attentions to war and valorous deeds (241-50).[8]

The character of Cassodorien is fascinating, even though she occupies a small part of the text. We are shown nothing of her own state of mind or plans, yet there are textual clues that something is fundamentally untrustworthy about this woman: Cassodorien is first

---

[8] In his *History of the Kings of Britain*, Geoffrey of Monmouth writes about Arthur's ascension after Uther's death that, "Arthur was a youth of fifteen years, of remarkable valor and generosity, whose natural goodness displayed such grace that he was loved by virtually all the people" (Loomis 64).

encountered in a liminal space. Whereas Melusine was found in the forest (a romance motif signifying of danger) Cassodorien is on a seafaring ship. According to Bjørn Thomassen, "liminality emerges in the in-between of a passage" (2). Thomassen thinks of liminality beyond just physical borders: he takes the idea of liminality further in terms of people (individuals, social groups, entire societies) and time (moments, periods, and epochs) which complicates the simple "between here and there" of the liminal space (89). Liminal spaces in terms of geography are not just the places in-between but also tend to be the strange places outside of the structures and customs of civilization.[9] Thus, it stands to reason the figures encountered while traveling through these spaces should be treated with caution because they are also liminal and outside traditional hierarchies. These figures are not in the human world, they are not quite in their own spaces either.[10] In terms of romance, a hero must be wary of the figures—particularly the female figures—he encounters while traveling through the wilderness. Henry's men find Cassodorien physically traveling by sea (a dangerous place in between lands and cultures) from Antioch to England.

Second, when we first meet Cassodorien she is surrounded by unimaginable, verging on the impractical, wealth. Before we meet her properly, we are treated to a detailed examination of the ship she sails on, which is given to be the height of luxury:

---

[9] A modern example of this kind of liminality would be an abandoned shopping mall, or an empty school or workplace at night after everyone has gone home. Places outside of their usual context become liminal.

[10] Encounters in liminal spaces, particularly the woods through which the heroes are traveling, are the bread and butter trope of the romance, and the following are well known cases: Both Sir Gromer Sumer Jour and Dame Ragnell are found by heroes traveling through the woods; the loathly lady of Chaucer's *Wife of Bath's Tale* is found dancing with faeries in a meadow (not to mention that the *Canterbury Tales* overall happens in the liminal space of pilgrimage); Orfeo finds the faerie hunting party riding in the woods; Lanval has his first meeting with his mistress when he sulking in the woods by a stream; Lancelot is abducted by the four Queens when he is napping under a tree in Malory; Yvain goes mad and lives like a naked wild man in the woods for a time; Robin Hood and other outlaws live in the woods, outside of the law and civilization; and even non-medieval fairy tales such as Red Riding Hood and Hansel and Gretel happen in the woods. The moral of the story—the woods are a terrifying place of (mis)adventure and we should probably stay out of them.

> Another schip they countryd thoo,
> Swylk on ne seygh they never non;
> All it was whyt of huel-bon,
> And every nayl with gold begrave:
> Off pure gold was the stave;
> Her mast was yvory;
> Off samyte the sayl wytterly.
> Her ropes wer off tuely sylk,
> Al so whyt as ony mylk.
> That noble schyp was al without,
> With clothys of golde spred aboute;
> And her loof and her wyndas,
> Off asure forsooth it was. (*RCL* 60-72)

The descriptions of the ship—the silk and samite, the gold, the dyed colors, the ivory, all have heavy Middle Eastern and eastern connotations. A little further on in the text, Henry II's men are invited aboard the ship and encounter the king seated in a chair of "charbocle ston" (89) and tablecloths of silk (103). Considering the expense of silk and the prestige of silk clothing, the use of silk tablecloths which are guaranteed to be dirtied and ruined shows an extravagance of wealth. In fact, there is nothing about this ship that is not extravagant: the masts are not made of wood but of ivory, the ropes are made of silk, the nails are gold, and the ship is presented as a sumptuous, bright, gold-gilded court on the sea. Jane Burns, in *Courtly Love Undressed*, examines the way identity is transmitted through cloth and clothing in French romance, and includes a lengthy discussion of Saracen silk and the wealth of Eastern products. It is very clear from the description of the ship and its inhabitants, that they are meant to be of Eastern origin. In her work, Burns notes,

> Even though after the mid-eleventh century many European countries could grow silk and make silk cloth, no European products rivaled the quality of Byzantine silks. Western copies, which imitated Byzantine and Muslim motifs and designs, remained inferior, since Byzantine silk production techniques were not fully known in the west. (191)

The sheer wealth described in the text makes it clear that these are not inferior quality European silks adorning Cassodorien's ship. Whether or not we believe that Cassodorien and her father are royalty of Antioch as they claim, indications of the Byzantine Empire are present (*RCL* 165).

This display of extravagance is a glaring clue that something is not right about Cassodorien, and hints at her supernatural nature from the very beginning. Encounters with the supernatural and with faeries in other medieval lays and romances use a similar overindulgence of material goods to highlight the Otherness of the faerie. Consider *Sir Orfeo*. When Orfeo follows the faerie hunting party from the forest into their own lands, he encounters a land of perfect summer beauty and a gigantic Otherworldly castle as unrealistically adorned with gold and jewels as Cassodorien's ship. An astonished Orfeo sees,

> The butras com out of the diche,
> Of rede gold y-arched riche—
> The vousour was avowed al
> Of ich maner diverse aumal;
> Within ther wer wide wones,
> Al of precious stones—
> The werst piler on to biholde
> Was al of burnist gold.
> Al that lond was ever light;
> For when it schuld be therk and night
> The riche stones light gonne
> As bright as doth at none the sonne. (361-72)

The castle Orfeo sees is literally made of gold and gemstones. The buttresses are red gold, the artwork inside and out of the castle buildings is painted with colorful enamels (363-4), and the poet notes that even the worst pillar was still made of burnished gold (368). If that description were not fabulous enough, the poet notes that the treasure castle glowed at night, radiating enough light that it shone as brightly at midnight as though it were midday. This impractical display of wealth means that Orfeo is a mortal who has strayed (albeit intentionally) into the faerie Otherworld. No mortal ruler, no matter how rich, could build such an immense structure of precious metal and jewels.

Sir Orfeo is not alone in connecting wealth to the supernatural; *Sir Launfal* does much the same. The pavilion where Launfal encounters his soon-to-be faerie mistress is extravagantly displayed, and the poet draws our attention to the golden eagle that adorns the whole structure. The figurine is encrusted with gems, and the poet says, "Alysaundre the conquerour, / Ne Kyng Artour yn hys most honour, / Ne hadde noon swych juell" (274-76). In other words, this description of a jewel beyond the reach even of Alexander or Arthur belongs merely to the tent-topper, not something of particular or sentimental worth. The pavilion is but the start of the treasures of *Sir Launfal*. The faerie mistress gives Launfal a bottomless purse of silk (319-24), the mistress's servants are clothed in samite (889), and the breast-strap of her palfrey alone is worth an entire earldom (958-9). Furthermore, the very end of the lay sees Launfal and his lady riding off into the sunset together and taking up residence in the land of Faerie (1035).

In sum, encounters with figures in liminal spaces and displays of ostentatious, impractical wealth function as short-hand for supernatural or magical origins. We may safely consider ourselves warned that whatever Cassodorien seems to be on the surface is not the uncomplicated truth of her. From the beginning, she possesses too many markers of the supernatural to be a mortal human woman. If these clues are not enough, the poet gets particularly direct, since Cassodorien freely admits to being unable to receive the Eucharist or even see the Mass performed: "I dar never see no sacrament" (*RCL* 194). No explanation is given for her avoidance and swooning reaction to the sacrament of the Eucharist, until she flies away. Yet, Cassodorien's relationship to Christianity is never questioned (at least not until the very end of her part in the text) and there is no talk of any necessary conversions before her marriage.

The English take for granted that the mysterious woman, despite hailing from the borderlands of the Latin East, is indeed Christian herself. Geographically, Antioch existed on the southernmost border of the Byzantine Empire. John Man writes, "Antioch was in Christian eyes second only to Jerusalem itself in wealth, size, strength and significance—St. Peter its first Patriarch, St. Paul a citizen. Once upon a time it had been Asia's greatest city (90). Located near the coast of the Mediterranean and a hop-skip from the island of Cyprus, Antioch was a major commercial center. It was seized by Christian forces during the First Crusade and existed in a delicate balance between the Byzantine emperor in Constantinople to the north and Jerusalem to the farther south, Jerusalem itself ruled by a Christian king (91). Complicating matters further, relations between the Latin East and the Latin West were generally fractious. The Byzantines existed in a religious borderland between the Latin (Roman) Church on the one side and the Muslims and Turks on the other. Before Rome became the seat of the Church, it had first made its capitol in Constantinople. After the move, the two halves of the Church existed uneasily together, with minor squabbling. However, by 1054, the squabbling resulted in the Byzantine Patriarchate and Roman Pope finally losing their tempers and excommunicating each other (Runciman 213). The Byzantine and Roman Church reconciled when Urban II lifted the ban on the Emperor in 1089 (prior to his call for the First Crusade in a scant six years' time), and both sides enjoyed a moment of tranquility. Yet, the open secret was that the thirty-plus years apart[11] had been enough to cause each side

---

[11] There is some contention on this point. See Peter Charanis's essay, "Aims of the Medieval Crusades and How They Were Viewed by Byzantium" in *Church History*. Prior to the reconciliation of the Latin and Byzantine churches he estimates that closer to 70 years had passed with very limited, if any, communion between the churches. In his notes, (#18) he mentions that the relationship between the two had been cold years before the

of the Church to evolve differently. Steven Runciman notes as much when he mentions that the paperwork for any reintegration was not completed because "the technicality of adding the pope's name to the official diptychs of the patriarchate was never made, as the pope never performed the necessary preliminary act of sending a Systatic letter to Constantinople declaring his faith—presumably because he did not want to raise any theological issue" (213). In any case, the good relationship barely lasted a decade. For their part, the crusaders—raised in the Latin West under the regimented and monolithic Catholic faith—had a certain amount of culture shock in the Byzantine, which was mostly tolerant of differing religious branches of the church and liturgical practices. After all, they had the Latins to the West, the Slavs to the North, and the Turks to the East, and in the crossroads of all of it, they learned to adapt to various liturgies. This tolerance was alien to the crusaders who were "used to one uniform ritual and was puzzled and shocked by any other ritual ... [the] services in the oriental churches seemed strange and hardly Christian" (Runciman 216). The wariness would continue, until the relationship between the Latins and the Byzantines eventually imploded with the sack of Constantinople in 1204 during the Fourth Crusade. And yet, regardless of any suspicion Latin Christianity might harbor for Eastern Christianity, in the romance, Henry and his court seem willing to accept the princess of Antioch as she presents herself without too many questions.

Still, it is hard to avoid the question of why the poet uses a Middle Eastern connection, instead of a more homegrown faerie or demon like Melusine. After all, a mysterious Scottish or French princess would do just as well if the poet is merely angling for exoticism. In her *Fantasies of the Other's Body in Middle English Oriental Romance*, Anna

---

mutual excommunications, although no one knows exactly when the relationship soured. For my purposes here, 1054 works as an official date to start from.

Czarnowus similarly notes, "In contrast to Melusine, [Cassodorien] is 'oriental' by origin, but Frenchness ... could make her equally exotic" (73). Considering England's fraught relationship with France and its experience with French foreign queens, notably the astute and wily Eleanor of Aquitaine herself as well as Edward II's treacherous wife Isabella, who gained the sobriquet of the "She-Wolf of France," the romance could easily have made Cassodorien a western French princess, but it seems important to the poet that Cassodorien be of eastern and demonic heritage, instead.

I argue that both eastern and demonic heritage are integral to legitimizing both Richard's crusading in the Middle East and his own barbaric behavior in the romance. If he gained his crown and royal prerogative to do as he wills because he is at the top of the English hierarchy, he gains his ability to crusade and operate outside the standards of his own culture from his Byzantine demon-mother. This emphasis on heritage comes around again much later in the text when Saladin sends a messenger to deliver a personal challenge to Richard for combat: "Thou cravyst heritage in this land. / And [Saladin] doos thè wel to undyrstand / That thou hast therto no ryght!" (5451-3) The word choice of "heritage" is telling, particularly when followed up by an emphatic insistence that Richard has no "ryght," which I take to mean that Richard has no legitimate or recognized claim to the land. Saladin could have used another word to emphasize control, dominion, or the conquering of the land, all things that Richard clearly wants. In the context of opening communication with a crusading European king, any other word would make sense. But the definition of "heritage" according to the Middle English Dictionary is,

> 1a. Something legally inherited or inheritable; inherited or inheritable property, right, office, sovereignty, etc....3a. (a) The fact or right of inheriting; hereditary succession, inheritance; bi (of) ~, bi name (laue, right, title, wei) of ~; of ~ bi kinde, by natural inheritance; of right(ful~), by lawful

inheritance, etc.; (b) hereditary possession or tenure; in (into, to) ~, by hereditary tenure, as an inheritance; in(to fe and ~, out of ~.

RCL is a romance intensely concerned with matters of nationalism, national identity, and yes, heritage. Through Cassodorien, Richard inherits a foothold in the East. For the poet, Richard is not simply crusading for the sake of crusading—Richard, as a son of a princess from Antioch, is taking land that he believes he has a legitimate stake in. The distinction makes all the difference. The poet uses Cassodorien to establish Richard not as a warmonger, but as a disinherited prince taking back his own. Furthermore, if Pope Urban II's speech is any indication, the contention in the Middle East often centered on who controlled Jerusalem and who had the right of heritage to Jerusalem (religiously and culturally), arguments which are still echoed in contemporary struggles over Jerusalem.

In the same message, Saladin offers Richard a horse of peerless value which Richard accepts, not knowing at the time that the horse is one of two demons conjured up to sabotage him (5491-99). The demons are a mother-son pair; between all the discussion of heritage and the appearance of related demons, it is hard to miss the association of the demon dam and colt with Richard's own demonic nature inherited from his mother. Yet Richard masters the exceptional demonic colt (a mirror of himself) and employs the demon in the service of the greater good and God:

> "Be the aposteles twelve,
> Though thou be the devyl hymselve,
> Thou schalt me serve at this need!
> He that on the rood gan blede,   5550
> And suffryd grymly woundes fyve,
> And sethen rose from deth to lyve,
> And boughte mankynd out off helle,
> And, sithen, the fendes pousté gan felle,
> And affiyr fleygh up into hevene,
> Now God, for hys names sevene,
> That is on God in Trinité,
> In hys name I comaunde thè

> That thou serve me at wylle!"—
> He schook hys hed and stood full stylle. (5547-60)

The horse might have been conjured up with a specific purpose to fulfill, but Richard binds the demon-horse to him instead. The binding is an odd detail, considering that the angel's instructions on the matter are more about tying a tree to the demon colt's mane and making sure Richard uses a good bridle, otherwise the angel merely directs Richard to "Ryde upon hym in Goddes name" (5508-33, 5523). The wording Richard uses for the binding is a rough approximation of the Apostle's Creed[12] which is a brief summarization of Christian theology. The Creed mentions, among many other things, Christ's suffering and death, descent into hell, rise from the dead, ascent into heaven, all things Richard specifically mentions, even if the elements he refers to are selective and out of order. Then Richard quickly veers into Old Testament territory with the seven names of God before whirling back around to the New Testament and finishing with an invocation of the Trinity. The overall effect of Richard's binding sounds impressive at first glance, but a closer examination reveals a haphazard, magpie's nest of theology, suggesting that Richard might not know exactly what he is talking about, but perhaps knows just enough to get the job done. For example, he mentions the seven names of God, but never actually recites any of them. One would think that if he wanted to be sure of binding the demon to his will, and if he wanted the demon to be sure that Richard was truly riding in God's name, that Richard would be more specific in his wording. For all that he claims to fight in God's name, takes the cross in terms of crusading and armor, and although he is visited by angels who warn him of treachery, we never actually

---

[12] According to Piotr Ashwin-Siejkowski in *The Apostle's Creed and Its Early Christian Context*, the Creed's "first appearance in its current form was in the eighth century, and the final Latin formula dates from the sixteenth century" (4). It is very likely that the poet and audience both would be familiar with at least some version of the Creed, as it is a staple tradition for every Mass.

see him in church. The scene where Cassodorien flees the Mass (207-34) neglects to mention whether Richard was even there himself. We assume he is, but we do not actually have textual evidence of it.

The demonic mare and colt are summoned by Saladin's necromancer (5490). Saladin plans to keep the dame and send the colt to Richard, knowing that when the mare neighed, the colt would come running to suckle. The plan is a clever one, even if it does violate basic equine husbandry:

> Was never kyng ne knyght so bolde,
> That, whenne the dame neyghe wolde,
> Scholde hym holde agayn hys wylle,
> That he ne wolde renne her tylle,
> And knele adoun, and souke hys dame:
> That whyle, the Sawdon with schame,
> Scholde Kyng Richard soone aquelle. (5501-7).

Setting aside the common-sense knowledge that any colt big enough to ride into battle would have long been weaned from its mother, the plan is to gift Richard with a horse pre-programmed to bring him conveniently within the Sultan's reach. The plan fails because, as discussed above, an angel visits Richard the night before and tells him how to tame the colt (5508-35). The demon dam-colt mirrors Cassodorien and Richard. Richard tames the demon-colt to do his will and God's work, but Richard himself (referred to as a devil throughout the romance) is also tamed and honed into a weapon for God. The fate of the demon-mare is also tellingly ambiguous. Cassodorien disappears from the text, and so does the mare after Richard engages the Sultan hand-to-hand and breaks the physical bindings of the mare's bridle and saddle:

> Brydyl and peytrel al to-brast;
> Hys gerth, and hys stiropes also;
> The mere to the grounde gan go.
> Mawgry hym he garte hym stoupe,

>Backward over hys meres croupe;
>The feet toward the firmament. (5732-37)

This passage is unsatisfying and raises more questions than it answers regarding the dam. Richard's blows destroy the mare's tack, and in line 5734 it sounds like the mare is beginning to either stumble or fall, even though the text does not mention a mortal blow being delivered to the horse itself. Line 5736 instead shows us the Sultan being violently unseated, falling or being pushed backward to the ground by Richard's spear, over the horse's rear end. This is the last time we see the demon-mare. She disappears from the text entirely, and we do not know if Richard killed the mare, if she simply threw and abandoned her rider, or if she disappeared into the ether from whence the necromancer conjured her. The next time we see Saladin himself, he is fleeing into the trees where Richard cannot follow because he has a forty-foot tree strapped to his horse (5803). Regardless, the demon mother/mare ultimately disappears from the text, leaving the demon son/colt behind to carry on God's work.

In sum, Cassodorien might only appear in the text for a brief time, but her supernatural origins reverberate through the entire text long after she has flown away from the church. She is coded supernaturally from before we even properly meet her through her appearance in a liminal space and otherworldly wealth, and her lineage as both a demon and princess of Antioch ultimately lends Richard's crusading endeavors legitimacy—including his unconventional foodways.

Cannibalism, Part I

Before discussing the text's first instance of cannibalism, I must briefly contextualize the foodways surrounding religion and pork, since it is Richard's demand for pork in the

Middle East that ultimately leads to cannibalizing Saracens. Foodways are inextricable from culture and identity, and are often part of unconscious habits:

> The act of ingestion and digestion involves the incorporation of food into our own flesh. What we eat literally becomes us, and we become it. Logically, therefore, food is among the most powerful expressions of identity, both for the individual and the group ... How we eat, what we eat, and with whom are the most fundamental reflections of who we are physically, emotionally, and spiritually. (Albala 7)

In other words, foodways are culturally coded. Cuisine and our mealtime companions not only reflect who we are and where we come from, but also how we wish to be perceived by others. Food choice reflects religion, ethnicity, personal ethical concerns, and class. A willingness to try foods from different places and cultures can even serve as a signifier for our own travels, wealth, interests, and personalities.

Food and Christianity had an uneasy relationship in the Middle Ages. While Christianity did not subscribe to the same strict food restrictions and concerns about (un)cleanliness of certain foods as did Judaism and Islam, the Church instead controlled what could be eaten *when*. In *Fast and Feast: Food in Medieval Society,* Bridget Ann Henisch discusses medieval foodways in detail. Fast days, also called fish days, comprised of approximately half the liturgical calendar year, with regular weekly fast days on Wednesdays, Fridays, and Saturdays, and special fasts for Lent and Advent. Apart from Lent, wherein Christians endured a near-vegan diet for forty days (no meat, eggs, or dairy, although fish was acceptable), the only major adjustment made for fast days was in the substitution of fish for meat. Even the amount of food prepared and consumed was normal although the ingredients were restricted. Food is an instrument of power, not only over others but also over oneself, so fasting was a way to practice and bolster self-discipline for the good of the soul (Henisch 7). Interestingly, medieval Christians may not have considered pride the worst of all sins. Satan might have been cast out of heaven for his presumption and pride, but that was his own mistake. Medieval Christians may have been more concerned about the fallibility of humanity than of angels-turned-demons, and concluded that Eden was lost not for pride, but for gluttony: Adam and Eve ate their way out of Eden by consuming the fruit from the Tree of Knowledge (Cosman 117). The complicated relationship with food is further revealed in the very Mass itself. In *Fabulous Feasts: Medieval Cookery and Ceremony*, Madeleine Pelner Cosman writes,

> Gluttony was the most simplistic explanation for sin in this world and man's temptation to it. Conversely, it was the most complex: the sacramental act of eating the body and blood of Christ had its perfect parallel, its special urgency, and its graphic vividness as an undoing, by eating, of an evil deed caused by eating. As Adam ate his way to sin, so man might eat his way to salvation. (120)

It is no wonder, then, why feast and fast were such preoccupations. Eating was at once the method of humanity's descent into sin, and of humanity's redemption from the same. Humans cannot physically live without eating, however, eating and the threat of gluttony was inherently dangerous to the soul. The struggle between the body and soul was most visceral in relation to food, and no one had a clear answer about how much should be eaten. At least with Judaism and Islam, the rules of food were clear regarding what could be consumed. For Christianity, the struggle over food was an unending matter of debate, ranging from what kinds of foods could be included on a Lenten menu to how much food should be eaten. Henisch notes that some heretical branches of Christianity, including the Cathars, took fasting to such extremes that some of them slowly starved themselves to death, to the approbation of their peers who admired their commitment to the cause of subduing the body in favor of the spirit (7).

Regardless of how much medieval Christianity knew (or did not know) about Islam, generally Muslims and Jews were often placed in the same category of Otherness, even if they were understood to be separate religions. Geraldine Heng notes that Christians did not often bother differentiating between Judaism and Islam, "as if the two infidel nations were halves of a single body of aliens" (82). After all, the Fourth Lateran Council of 1215 required all Jews *and* Muslims to wear distinctive clothing to mark them as Other and prevent cultural or religious contamination of Christians. Regarding obvious foodways, according to Daphne Barak-Erez, the Jewish prohibition against pork was a well-known fact "that other nations exploited ... to oppress the Jews" (18). An example of such an exploitation is that in fifteenth century Spain and Portugal, converted Jews were required to publicly eat pork as proof of their conversion, particularly during the Inquisition (Barak-Erez 21). Considering that the Jews and Muslims had some similar foodways, the Christian imagination was readily able to conflate the two.

Both Judaism and Islam had strict prohibitions regarding pork, although the Judaic reasons for the prohibition are many and lack consensus, including but not limited to the fact that swine have multiple births whereas most accepted animals have one or two offspring at a time (Ruane 494). Another concern, according to Ken Albala, is the diet that pigs keep. Swine are omnivores that eat garbage and other unclean things. Albala writes, "Quite simply the rule to eat only animals which chew their cud and have a cloven hoof was intended to be a short hand way of recognizing ruminants, those untainted by murder, which we must recall was forbidden since the time of Eden. The sin of carnivorous animals is unexpiated by sacrifice, and thus they are unclean" (Albala 10). Because swine have been known to kill and eat small animals without a cleansing or sacrificial ritual, they are not strict herbivores and are considered unclean. Still more theories focus on economics and natural resources that made pig-breeding unsuitable to the Middle East: "Pigs need shade, and area in which to wallow in mud or water, and food much richer than the grass provided to animals that chew the cud" (Barak-Erez 16). Conditions for raising pigs are much better in Europe where such things are readily available, but the Middle East is inhospitable to swine (who are even susceptible to sunburn, hence the wallowing in mud) and thus, pigs would not be cost effective to raise. A colleague of mine who is a knowledgeable and practicing Muslim also mentioned that Muslims have strict standards regarding the humane treatment of livestock both before and during the slaughter. *Halal* customs prohibit the consumption of blood, meaning animals must be bled out completely. Unfortunately, there is no easy or humane way to bleed a pig. Thus, to avoid cruelty, pork is considered unclean meat and thus not permitted (*haram*).[13]

In any case, the poet of *RCL* was certainly aware that there were plenty of mitigating reasons why pork would be impossible to find in the Middle East, but the English army's desperate search for it leads to two of the most famous scenes of *RCL*: the king's cannibalism of Saracens. The first instance of cannibalism takes Richard entirely by surprise. When he falls ill, all he desires is pork. After all his travel through unfamiliar climates and eating unfamiliar foods, the Christian English king craves a meat that cannot be found anywhere in the country, no matter how far they range and how insistent the king is that they find him pork:

> To mete hadde he no savour,
> To wyn, ne watyr, ne no lycour;
> But afftyr pork he was alonged.
> But, though hys men scholde be hongyd,
> They ne myghte, in that cuntree,
> For gold, ne sylvyr, ne no monee,
> No pork fynde, take, ne gete,
> That King Richard myght ought off eete. (3047-54)

---

[13] Special thanks to Dylan Charpentier, who patiently answered my questions about Islamic foodways. See also, "What is Halal? A Guide for Non-Muslims" by the Islamic Council of Victoria, for more general information on *halal* practices.

At first, the situation seems dire, but closer examination of the passage speaks more about Richard's character than any supposed illness. First, "to mete he had no savour / to wyn, ne watyr, ne no lycour" does not mean that Richard was incapable of eating or that he had a shortage of food that would lead to illness. It means that once he decided he wanted to eat pork—a highly unreasonable request, considering his current location in the Middle East—he essentially refused to eat or drink until his whim was fulfilled. In his craving for pork, nothing else tasted good, so he would not consume it. In the middle of a campaign, the king is willing to send his men, under the threat of execution should they fail ("though hys men scholde be hongyd"), to search the country to see if there is any pork they can beg, buy, or outright steal. Furthermore, it is well known that humans can go up to a week without food, but for Richard to also refuse to drink hints at a certain level of manipulative despotism.

Eventually, an older knight talks to Richard's steward, and informs the man that no matter how hard they try, no one is going to find actual pork for the king to consume— something they all know but no one is brave enough to actually tell the king plainly for fear of death: "No man be hardy hym so to telle! / Yiff he dede he myght deye" (3062-3). The threat of hanging in the earlier passage was neither a joke nor an overstatement. These lines reinforce the king's willingness to execute anyone who tells him no, and his retinue all believe his threat to hang them. However, the old knight has an unorthodox solution to their problem:

> Take a Sarezyne yonge and fat;
> In haste that the theff be slayn,
> Openyd, and his hyde off flayne,
> And sodden ful hastely,
> With powdyr and with spysory,
> And with saffron off good colour. (3066-71)

Scholars do not seem to pay much attention to the old knight who suggests cannibalism. Overshadowed by the cannibalistic episode itself, the character who only briefly steps forward to offer advice and who disappears from the text afterward does not inspire much interest. However, his instructions to the steward are oddly specific, down to the spices the cook should use to flavor the meat: "With powdyr and with spysory, / and with saffron[14] off good colour" (3069-70). I suggest, then, that the knight is evidence of prior cannibalism which has happened off-page. Otherwise, how would the old knight know how to prepare the meat? If we examine the specific, step-by-step advice the old knight provides, we are struck by the sheer outlandishness of the situation. Richard's people are afraid to inform him that there is no pork to be found in the country because they might lose their heads, but they *are* willing to feed him human flesh.

The key to understanding this absurdity may be found if we look away from foodways for a moment and consider humor as another effective tool of identity-creation. In *Empire of Magic*, Geraldine Heng argues that the cannibalism in *RCL* is less about food and more about perpetuating an aggressive nationalistic joke. She writes,

> what defines the Englishman—the national subject—is his delight in eating up the natives in his march of conquest into foreign—international—territory. As Richard gleefully mimes that foreign aggression through a cannibalistic joke, he perceptibly conjures up a national collectivity of souls, materializes a unity of Christian Englishmen whose extraterritorial gustatory habits define their very identity. (74)

The initial instance of cannibalism is a joke played on Richard by his own courtiers who know exactly what—or who—the king is greedily devouring: "And whenne he hadde eaten

---

[14] Saffron is a spice from southern Europe, the Middle East, and Asia. It is often used as a flavor enhancer for both sweet and savory dishes and can be used as a food colorant (particularly rice) for its yellow-gold color. Saffron is still expensive. For a survey of medieval European recipes that make use of saffron and many other spices, see *Pleyn Delit: Medieval Cookery for Modern Cooks*, by Constance Hieatt, Sharon Butler, and Brenda Hosington.

inowgh, / Hys folk hem turnyd away and lowgh" (*RCL* 3091-2). Richard's court watches him consume human meat and instead of feeling horrified by the sight, they suppress laughter. Presumably, they felt secure in their monarch's sense of humor to think they could get away with feeding their unwitting king a Saracen, and they are correct. After a moment of stunned silence following the reveal of the Saracen's head, Richard's reaction to finding out what/who they had fed him is uproarious laughter: "[he] gan to laughe as he wer wood" (3191). Humor is a tool of community-building and boundary-setting because laughter demarcates who is "in" the group and who is outside of it: "[w]ith laughter, the audience signals acceptance of the joker's invitation to join him or her in the humorous mode of discourse for the time being" (Smith 152). Laughing signifies a set of shared values between speaker and audience, whereas not-laughing, or unlaughter[15] signifies the opposite. The English find Richard's cannibalism funny, and so does he.

Cannibalism, Part II

A practical joke is one thing, but Richard takes the cannibalism a step further in not only approving of the consumption of human meat but also using it as a weapon. He immediately plans a nightmarish dinner party for a diplomatic delegation of Saracens who want to negotiate the return of Saracen prisoners (3388-3414). Heng notes the way Richard turns the initial joke against himself into one against the Saracens themselves: "Richard's mastery of ideological manipulation is glimpsed in how deftly he turns an initially affectionate joke against himself, in the first cannibalism, into a collective hostile joke

---

[15] "Unlaughter" is a term coined by Michael Billig in *Laughter and Ridicule*. Unlaughter functions as a rhetorical device. More than just being a state of not-laughing, unlaughter is a very pointed absence of laughter in a situation where laughter is a hoped-for outcome by a speaker, and it works as an expression of strong outrage or disapproval (192). Usually, unlaughter happens when the audience finds a joke or remark offensive or otherwise disagreeable. While the English audience finds the king's cannibalism hilarious, the Saracens who witness him eating their kinsman in the second episode of cannibalism do not find the situation amusing at all.

against the enemy, in the second cannibalism—extrapolating, in the process, a community called 'England,' made up of 'good,' 'English,' 'Christian men' who are defined by their appetite for Muslims" (75). The joke itself, as much as their foodways, defines the cultural boundaries between the Christian English and the Muslim Saracens. However, the second episode of cannibalism complicates those cultural boundaries, even as it ostensibly sets them.

The romance seems to back away from approving of the cannibalism when it is intentional and provides the audience with an ambivalent presentation of the second instance of cannibalism. If the first instance of cannibalism was amusing in a macabre way, the second episode of cannibalism is deadly serious and seems to invite the audience to consider what it means to be human/not-human. Considering the romance as a whole, the text's constant referral to the Saracens as heathens, hounds, and devils calls into question the very humanity of the Saracens themselves. At best the romance treats Saracens as treacherous animals, and at worst, as a race of demons. By demonizing the Saracens, the romance undercuts the king's cannibalistic exploits. The romance suggests if Saracens are little better than the hounds they are referred to, then perhaps eating them is the equivalent of eating a dog—not necessarily palatable, but not worse than starving crusaders resorting to eating their horses and their entrails[16] when conditions were dire enough: "Then our good hors we

---

[16] In the *Itinerarium Peregrinorum et Gesta Regis Ricardi*, the famine crusaders endured was so great that a last resort was the slaughter and consumption of horses: "rather than let humans die while beasts of burden were spared, they slew their precious warhorses and consumed the horseflesh with pleasure, sometimes without having even skinned the animals first. A horse's offal was sold for ten shillings ... so they devoured the bodies of their mounts. Those who used to carry them, vice versa, they now carried in their stomachs. A horse was worth more dead than alive ... Such was the nature of famine that when they had slaughtered a horse none of the offal was regarded as waste; every part, no matter how vile, was greatly valued" (Nicholson 127-128). Considering the huge expense to buy, train, and keep warhorses, the fact that crusaders were killing and eating them underscores the desperation of the times, which is an interesting juxtaposition with Richard's dangerous petulance in demanding pork and disdaining all other foods available to him.

slowgh; / Dede sethe, and eete the guttys tough" (2825-26). Even Richard comments on the unexpected viability of eating Saracens when supplies get low:

> What is Sarezynys flesch thus good?
> That never erst I nought wyste!
> By Godes deth and hys up-ryste,
> Schole we never dye for defawte,
> Whyl we may, in any assawte,
> Slee Sarezynes, the flesch mow take,
> And sethen, and roste hem, and doo hem bake
> Gnawen her flesch to the bones.
> Now I have it proved ones,
> For hunger ar I be woo,
> I and my folk schole eet moo! (lines 3192-3202)

Simply put, Saracens are unexpectedly delicious to the king, and he wastes no time in turning this tidbit of knowledge to his best interests. Unlike the old knight, who considered cannibalism as a practical solution to the comparatively minor problem of his king's temper tantrum about pork, Richard admits that cannibalism never occurred to him, but now he considers cannibalism a viable measure to sustaining his troops. No more must the English fear dying of starvation or deprivation so long as there are Saracens to kill and cook. Nationalistically speaking, Richard realizes that his crusade is not only about the takeover and consumption of land and natural resources, but also of the Saracens too.

Richard utilizes cannibalism in his diplomatic endeavors, and the second episode of cannibalism follows very closely the first episode. Furthermore, as if witnessing the scene were not enough, the romance provides a recap of the entire affair, including the identities of the killed and cooked Saracens, in the first-hand account of one of the horrified dinner guests who reports back to Saladin (3540-3632). The king puts an unusual amount of thought into the presentation of the nightmarish dinner party and sends along special menu instructions via his steward. The joke that his own court had played on him, the king turns toward the Saracens. Granted, he does not allow them to unknowingly cannibalize their own kinsmen, but rather has the first course of cooked human heads served, labeled on the forehead so there is no doubt as to the identity of the victims, unaccompanied by any bread, salt, or wine (3423-4, 3436-39). Perhaps Richard did not have the patience to set up a long joke by inflicting cannibalism on his guests, or perhaps he simply had a flair for the dramatic, because when the first course is served, he simply eats the head set before him while his guests grieve their losses and look on in horror at Richard, who pretends nothing unusual is happening. In fact, like any host who notices reticent guests, he asks them if anything is wrong with the food: "Why kerve ye nought off your mese, / And eetes faste as I doo? / Tell me why ye louren soo?" (3468-70). When the feast is finally over, and Richard's guests beg leave to return home, Richard obliges but sends along a message for Saladin, informing him that the English will never worry about starving so long as there are Saracens available to cook:

> He says, and hys men make boost,
> He schal not leete on lyve,
> In al thy lond, man, chyld, ne wyve;
> But slee all that he may fynde,
> And seethe the flesch and with teeth grynde. (3624-29)

The warning is a grim one, as Richard is both relentless and ruthless, unwilling to spare anyone in his path. He and his company will not just eat men, but women and children as well. Nicola McDonald views the scene as a stroke of inspired, if macabre genius on Richard's part:

> Anthropophagic annihilation (the total consumption of a people) not only mirrors the crusaders' political and religious aspirations, as Heng argues, but fuels those aspirations (it provides the crusaders with the alimentary sustenance that is otherwise in short supply), and—if successful—guarantees the impunity of Christian hegemony ... Eating people makes an awful lot of pragmatic sense. (134)

Interestingly, it is the lack of cultural understanding and exchange that allows Richard to get away with his scheme: "The messangeres nought ne knewe / Richardys law ne hys custome" (lines 3418-19). Arguably, the success of the trick revolves around Richard's ability to convincingly play dumb when he claims that it is his custom to eat a first course of obviously human flesh and that he did not know his own guests' culinary customs (3485-89), but even so, the Saracens "wenden he hadde be wood" (3458). That line is a reminder of the similar line during first episode of cannibalism where Richard laughed at the joke as though he were mad. In the second episode, no one is laughing. The Saracen delegation is legitimately concerned that Richard is insane and are afraid of him: "They seten style and sore quook: / They durste neyther speke ne look" (3471-2). Because they are outside of the English community, they do not find Richard's trick amusing.

Taking Richard's own court's response to the first instance of cannibalism, I am convinced that the poet's English audience would find the cannibalism funny in both instances. The first episode is macabre, but the king's enthusiasm for his meal makes his court laugh:

> He eete faster than he karve myght.
> The kyng eet the flesh and gnew the bones,
> And drank wel afftyr, for the nones:
> And whenne he hadde eaten inowgh,
> Hys folk hem turnyd away and lowgh.
> He lay stylle, and drowgh in hys arme;
> Hys chaumberlayn hym wrappyd warm.
> He lay and slepte, and swette a stound,
> And become hool and sound. (3088-96).

Admittedly, the image of the king eating ravenously, gnawing on bones, and then falling asleep at the table and being left to sleep off his meat sweats and sickness is funny. The English audience would take their cue to laugh from the in-text courtiers who try to smother their mirth. Like the courtiers, the listening audience is in on the joke; at this moment the king remains blissfully ignorant of his meal, but everyone witnessing the scene both inside and outside of the text are aware that he is eating human flesh. However, the second instance of cannibalism is only funny to part of the audience. Again, the English audience inside and outside of the text are in on the joke. The Saracen guests are not in on the joke and demonstrate terrified unlaughter. They return to Saladin and report the events of the meal with the king and the unlaughter is made doubly obvious in their recounting of their terror: "For drede hou we begunne to quake" (3595). Of course, the heads of the slain and cooked Saracens are known to the horrified dinner guests because they are kin and labelled to ensure recognition (3568-80). Saladin's delegation was served the heads of the very men they wanted to ransom from Richard. From the Saracen point of view, there is nothing amusing about being presented with the cooked heads of their friends and kinsmen. In this scene, the boundaries between the English and the Saracens are clearly demarcated by humor. Richard parodies the role of a good host by playing dumb to Saracen social mores as he publicly cannibalizes one of his Saracen captives, but the Saracens are not laughing. The English's macabre joke is on them, and their response is terror.

The Marble King

Throughout the romance, Richard's demonic heritage complicates and blurs the boundaries between the English and the Saracens. If the Saracens at his table are devils (Richard himself calls them such when the head of his "swine" is revealed, line 3190) and not entirely human, then the English king, by his mother's demonic nature, is not entirely human himself. The Saracens at Richard's table think he is related to the devil, "the devel's brothir" (3460), an idea later echoed by Saladin's court when they hear of the grotesque feast: "Herde we never swylke mervayle. / It is a devil withouten fayle" (*RCL* 3639-40). Interestingly, the Saracens are not the first to call Richard "a devyl, and no man" (498). That distinction belongs to his own English companions. Overall, the king's demonic nature is difficult to parse. On the one hand, everyone—regardless of English or Saracen identities—refers to Richard as a devil. It is not a hard leap to make, considering his demonic mother, Cassodorien. On the other hand, there are instances of divine intervention by way of an angel appearing to warn him of Saladin's treachery, and Richard's mastery of the demonic horse gifted to him from Saladin (5508-09). The angel's help complicates Richard's identity of being part demon and suggests that without this divine intervention (which he depends on) he would have failed. Demonic heritage and cannibalistic tendencies aside, the text clearly shows that Richard still has the hand of God on him, and his cause is divinely ordained.

The end of the romance further confuses Richard's supernatural nature, because for most of the poem Richard is called a devil by the English and by the Saracens. However, in the twilight sections of the romance, not only is Richard experiencing angelic visitations that serve as divine warnings of Saracen treachery, but even the epithets used to describe him begin to include words suggesting angels or sainthood. As the narrative meanders to a conclusion, it becomes clear that the poet is adding a small redemptive story arc—one that requires Richard winning not just land and cities for the greater glory of England, but winning souls to Christianity. After thousands of lines of warfare and psychological intimidation tactics, the audience is presented with a small, comedic episode wherein Richard makes a wager for the souls of a town.

The episode begins with Richard, fresh from his victory of taking the city of Daroun, marching on the city of Gatrys. The city's lord is a man who was once a mighty warrior in his prime, but is now elderly:

> He that was lord off Gatris,
> Hadde ben a man off mekyl prys.
> And fel to fyght ageyns hys foo;
> But that ilke tyme he was nought soo,

>For he was fallen in elde,
>That he myght non armes welde. (6173-78)

At first glance, the elderly Saracen seems to be described respectfully, as an old man who lived an active and chivalric life and who earned his place as a leader of men when he was at the height of his prowess. Yet, a closer examination of this description is as hollow and damning as any others in the romance that describe Saracens unfavorably as cowards or heathen hounds. The phrase that "he was fallen in elde" is interesting, because it seems to suggest that age is a disease or dishonor for the active warrior—and dying young or in battle is the best, most honorable ending. The subtext suggests that only cowards live to be elderly. This reading is further supported by the next action. For whatever reason, the elderly lord of the city is no longer physically able to defend his city against incursion, so he devises a bizarre solution:

>In myddes the toun, upon a stage,
>He leet make a marbyl ymage,
>And crownyd hym as a kyng,
>And bad hys folk, old and ying,
>That they scholde never be aknow
>To Crystene man, hygh ne low,
>That they hadde no lord off dygnyté,
>But that ymage in that cyté. (6180-8)

The solution contradicts the description of the lord as once a "man of mekyl prys" (6174). A truly brave man of reputation, regardless of age, would not create a marble statue (presumably of himself, although the text does not elaborate specifically), crown it, and tell his people to pretend that the statue is their lord. The irony in the last two lines is telling: first, it is true that the city lacks a dignified lord, because the man hides from danger when he is needed most; and second, his leadership is as empty and useless as the statue standing in the middle of the city.

Unlike Richard, who seems to find the entire situation of being confronted by the stone image of a leader hilarious, the lord of the city does not have the hand of God upon him, despite his image being in the company of Muhammad and Apollo. Richard offers to defeat the image, on the condition that if he wins they will all convert to Christianity. The statue is duly smote down, killing five Saracens standing under it (6226), and everyone converts: "Alle the othyr sayde than, / 'He was an aungyll and no man,' / And al become Crystene thore" (6227-9). Because Richard has been considered at least part devil for most of the romance, the sudden switch of his enemies-turned-Christians calling him an angel is a bit jarring. Of course, he is now winning souls for Christianity, so calling him a devil in this instance would be counterintuitive. Yet Richard, we well know, is not going to survive the end of the romance, so the poet begins the process not only of rebranding Richard as a symbol of English nationalism, but also of redeeming his soul, which gives the angelic visitations more credence as evidence of divine approval. Interestingly, the juxtaposition of Richard with the elderly lord of the city brings the romance back around to the very beginning. In the beginning of the romance the poet says he will read "off a kyng, doughty in dede; / Kyng Richard, the warrior best, / That men fynde in ony jeste" (30-33). The city's lord lived not just into old age but old age with infirmity. We know Richard will not get the chance because he is too "doughty in dede" and vigorous.

Richard's redemption is not the only function of this passage because it includes common stereotyping and misinformation about the Islamic religion. As mentioned above, the statue of the lord is accompanied by statues of Muhammad and Apollo, suggesting pagan idolatry. In *Sons of Ishmael*, John Tolan discusses the literary convention of medieval texts that paint Saracens as pagans and idolaters:

> Many Christian authors, from the eighth century to the sixteenth, depicted Saracens as idolatrous pagans. This image, familiar to us through the *Chanson de Roland* and other chansons de geste, is, according to some critics (in particular Norman Daniel), a mere literary convention, born of ignorance, which does not reflect the way that educated Europeans viewed Muslims and Islam. Yet recent studies have shown to what extent this portrait of the Saracen Other could be used to justify and glorify the violence of the warrior class; the Saracen Other reinforces the ideology of Christian knighthood. The story of Corbaran's conversion celebrates the crusader's exploits and anchors them in Christian history and eschatology. They become events in the perennial struggle between Christians and pagans, a struggle that is destined to end in Christian victory. (67)

Tolan is not discussing *RCL*, but the same ideas can be applied to Richard's conversion of Saracens. By including marble images of both Muhammad and Apollo, the poet utilizes a long-standing tradition common to crusading propaganda that paints Saracens as idolators and polytheists, worshipping empty signs and statues. Leona Cordery notes, "[t]he three most common [gods] are Termagaunt, Appolyn (clearly referencing Apollo) and Mahoun (a clear reference to the prophet Muhammad) …These gods are normally described as being represented in stone idols" (95). Richard demonstrates the inefficacy of Saracen gods by providing a "gret wundyr" (line 6210) by destroying the stone image of the city's lord. Summarily impressed by this feat of man vs. stone, the city's inhabitants agree to convert to Christianity and are thus spared the sword. The episode, which begins with the old lord and the town's inhabitants playing a joke on the Christian invaders, ends with Richard turning the joke to his own advantage and converting the entire town. Furthermore, the townspeople bring the elderly lord before Richard, who "lowgh with good entent, / And gaff hym the cyté to welde" (6234-5). The elderly lord is restored to his position by Richard, who finds the entire caper hilarious. The episode and the presentation of the Saracens are marginally less offensive in this instance because Richard is not meeting any military resistance and the locals are about to be converted to Christianity.

The Chivalric Saracen: Saladin

It would be remiss to end a chapter that discusses Richard I's Third Crusade exploits without also saying a brief word about Saladin, the Sultan of Egypt and Syria. Born in Tikrit, Mesopotamia as Yusuf ibn Ayyub, he was raised in the courts of Damascus under the tutelage of Nur ad-Din. He would later be called Salah ad-Din, or Saladin to Westerners (Reston 5). Saladin managed to do what might have been impossible a few generations earlier—unite most of the Arab world. James Reston notes that, "Only because of the divisions among petty potentates, because of the feud between the Islamic sects of the Sunnis and the Shi'ites and between competing caliphates in Egypt and Syria and Turkey had the First Crusade succeeded. But gradually, with a slow inevitability that was almost providential, the Arab world consolidated its power in the face of European occupation" (7). In other words, the First Crusade was a success because the Arab world was fractured, both religiously and politically. Saladin, by his takeovers of Egypt, Mesopotamia, Damascus, and Yemen, erased these barriers and established a Sunni Muslim empire equipped and capable of taking on the Christian crusader armies and, often, winning.

Generally, in both history and art, Saladin was (and continues to be) well-regarded by both the Arabic and the Christian world as a princely, chivalric knight:

> Saladin stands out in Western accounts of the Middle Ages because his beliefs and actions reflected supposedly Christian characteristics: honesty, piety, magnanimity, and chivalry. Unlike many Muslim rulers, he was not cruel to his subordinates; Saladin believed deeply in the Qur'ānic standard that all men are equal before the law. He set a high moral tone; for example, he distributed war booty carefully to help maintain discipline in the ranks. (Chase)

Saladin also had a reputation for being generous to his enemies—sometimes overly so, as proven by his capture and ransoming of Jerusalem. Originally, those who could pay the ransom would be freed from the captive Jerusalem, with the remaining poor to be sold off as slaves; however, he found excuses to free as many as possible. Reston writes, "Saladin's heart was not, however, in this traffic in human beings. He seemed amenable to all sorts of last-minutes special requests" (83). This courtesy was not limited to the captives he took but also to his enemies on and off the battlefield. Once, he gifted Richard with horses in the middle of a battle (Reston 292) and he sent fruit and ice when Richard was grievously ill (301). Saladin even appears in Dante's *The Divine Comedy*, as a resident of the first circle of hell, purgatory, which is designated for the worthy pagans and pre-Christians:

> To me the Master good: "Thou dost not ask
> What spirits these, which thou beholdest, are?
> Now will I have thee know, ere thou go farther,
> That they sinned not; and if they merit had,
> 'Tis not enough, because they had not baptism
> Which is the portal of the Faith thou holdest;
> And if they were before Christianity,
> In the right manner they adored not God;
> And among such as these am I myself.
> For such defects, and not for other guilt,
> Lost are we and are only so far punished,
> That without hope we live on in desire." (*Inferno*: Canto IV)

Saladin, the narrator says, sits alone, but in the overall august company of the geniuses of the ancient world—philosophers, mathematicians, royalty, poets, and military heroes (*Inferno*: Canto IV). The Guide points out that the reason those personages are in limbo is not because they were evil but that they were not baptized Christians. They may well even have served God, but because they did not do so properly (read: the Christian way) they were resigned to this circle of hell. They are not fit for heaven, but hell proper has no place for them, either.

The Saladin in the *RCL* is pale shadow of the historical man: by turns diplomat who offers Richard immense treasure and land for peace or prisoners (3213-26, 3339-51), coward who flees before Richard's might (3141, 5097-5110), and devious plotter. Throughout the romance, Saladin remains an almost distant character—we get more of Richard's point of view and thought process than we get of Saladin's. The historical Saladin was an even match for Richard in charisma and strategic brilliance, and quite possibly Richard's better in terms of generosity and gentility. The romance-Saladin is often foiled by Richard or seen running away from battle. Many times, he only appears for a few lines, usually as an interlude between battles or stratagems. The poet even re-writes one of Saladin's most gallant acts during the final battle of the Third Crusade. With the crusader troops exhausted, and only approximately a dozen horses remaining in the entire army, Richard fought beside his men on foot after his own horse was wounded (Man 222). The Sultan, impressed and moved by the English king's resilience, sends him a gift of two Arabian horses in the middle of the melee (Reston 291-92). The action was on par with any romance-knight's act of mercy or generosity.

The episode of the demonic mare and colt is again informative, this time about Saladin's character. Instead of two valuable Arabians, the horses in the romance are both conjured demons, and Saladin only offers Richard one of them (5462-68). He attempts to slay Richard with treason by gifting him a demonic colt but is himself demonized. There are a lot of demon references placed in one scene: Saladin is struck from his own demonic mare (the match for Richard's demonic colt) and left lying in the grass (5739). Once it becomes clear that the battle is going badly for the Saracens, Saladin retreats in despair:

> [Saladin] gan to flee al so sone,
> And fayn alle thoo that myght.
> And Kyng Richard, that noble knyght,
> Whenne he seygh the Sawdon fleygh
> "Abyde, coward!" he cryde on heygh,
> "And I schal thè proven fals,
> And thy cursyd goddess als."
> Kyng Richard dryves afftyr fast;
> The Sawdon was ful sore agast;
> A gret woode he before hym sees,

> Thedyr in fol haste he flees. (5790-5800)

The poet pokes fun at Saladin for retreating with the comment that Saladin "gan to flee al so sone" implying that Saladin does not remain to see the battle go against him but runs at the first sign of trouble. Furthermore, while Richard is associated with devils throughout the romance, this scene is particularly interesting in the way Saladin is depicted next to Richard. The word "fleygh" in line 5792 recalls Cassodorien's own flying escape from the church in the beginning of the romance. The English king, ostensibly of the demon's brood and riding a demon horse, is on the side of the angels whereas the sultan is depicted as the smooth-talking serpent in the garden of Eden: "In his blasoun, verryment, / Was i-paynted a serpent" (5727-29). This turn to a higher power is reflected in the positions of both characters: the sultan is fleeing into the woods on foot, but Richard is "on heygh" (5794). Not only does this scene invert history, where Saladin was seated on a horse watching his opponent fight on foot, but now Richard is literally higher: physically higher because he is on horseback, and morally higher through God's angelic intervention.

The end of the romance comes with Richard suing for peace in a truce: "thre yer, thre monethys, and thre dawes" (7104). Saladin agrees to the truce (7096-7116). This too, is an inversion of history. The result of the final battle at Jaffa was a stalemate and a peace treaty, not a temporary truce. Historically, it was Saladin who ended the crusade by offering Richard terms of peace, provided that the crusaders disarmed and surrendered a fortification called Ascalon. Richard initially refused, but the king's health was failing after such a long campaign. According to John Man, after the battle of Jaffa, Richard collapsed with a fever and Saladin sent the same overtures of peace a second time, accompanied by a chilled drink, peaches, and pears from his own supply (223). Richard was done. Man writes, "Richard could not go on. He was sick, his troops were tired and his brother John looked likely to seize the English throne …. On 2 September, he signed the Treaty of Jaffa, ending the Third Crusade, and so the next day did Saladin. It really was over at last" (223). The romance has a different ending: the indefatigable Richard does not give in because of exhaustion and illness so much as an understanding that his absentee rulership for so long has created an opportunity for his brother to take control (*RCL* 6267-6290). Richard decides to finish the crusade and then go home to war with John over England (6310-12). Historically, Saladin might have been Richard's equal, but throughout the romance the poet reimagines him as a coward to better elevate Richard who the romance claims "neuer was found coward" (4). Since the closing lines of the romance follow the fate of Richard, nothing more is said of Saladin.

Conclusion

Richard does not survive the romance. In the last thousand lines or so, we are informed that trouble is brewing in England because Prince John has usurped his brother's crown in his absence. The romance ends abruptly after Richard's temporary accord with Saladin:

> Kyng Richard, doughty off hand,
> Turnyd homeward to Yngeland.
> Kyng Richard reynyd here
> No more but ten yere.
> Sythe he was schot, alas! (7127-31)

The romance is not interested in Richard's life after he returns home—perhaps because continuing the tale in England would take even more of a suspension of disbelief than a king being an enthusiastic two-time cannibal. Historically, Richard's entire reign lasted ten years, although the ambiguous wording of the above passage is vague enough to mean that romance-Richard spent at least some or all that decade in England ("reynyd here") instead of the six months he historically resided there. Although, since Richard signed a truce for three years, it seems unlikely that he would remain a day longer in England when he could return to the Holy Land after subduing his seditious younger brother. Very little detail of Richard's return to England and death is included, beyond the information that he was shot at Gaylard Castle (7132). The poet has taken great pains to erase Richard's French identity and to build an English identity in his place, so the poet must take care about including details of Richard's grim fate defending his French holdings, lest all that work to rewrite Richard as the paragon of Englishness be undone. In the end, the romance remains a bastion of crusading propaganda, and English nationalism and identity, celebrating the fictional exploits of Richard over the Saracens in the Holy Land. The romance builds English identity in a multitude of ways, including using the English language, opposition to the French and the Saracens, foodways and cannibalism, and practical jokes and humor. Richard himself is defined by his demonic and ambiguously Middle Eastern heritage from his mother, Cassodorien. Although, like the demon colt Richard has been honed into an instrument of God, a tacit acknowledgement that to do God's will (crusading), sometimes one must implement the methods of the devil: war, violence, and cannibalism.

Chapter 2: Women and the Power of Conversion

Crusade romances are often meditations on ways to retake control of the Holy Land and the entirety of the Middle East. Military conquest is one method of conquering, but some romances consider a different approach: incorporation through conversion. This chapter focuses on the ways the Middle English romances *Firumbras*, *Bevis of Hampton*, and *The King of Tars* use Saracen and Christian women to legitimize Western crusading through the power of conversion. Some romances, like *Sir Isumbras* and *Richard Coer de Lion*, include the conversion of Saracens to Christianity, but they focus on forced conversion as a tactic. However, there is another way to facilitate Saracen conversions: love. The Saracen princess invariably converts for romantic love as part of her wooing and winning her Christian lover, whereas the Christian damsel may help convert an entire nation by converting her Saracen husband. Connecting women to religious conversion has some very gendered implications in the way that power is gained, lost, or wielded. On the one hand, the conversion of the Saracen princess, like Josian or Floripas, although considered suspect because she converts to Christianity for love of a Christian knight rather than any demonstrated conviction to Christian values, legitimizes colonialism. Not only have the Christian knights invaded the Middle East on crusade, ostensibly to "liberate" the Holy City of Jerusalem described in feminine terms by Pope Urban II in his call to arms at the Council of Clermont,[17] but in addition to taking land and cities, they have seduced the women of the highest degree. For the Christian knights, conversion of their beloved to Christianity is a non-negotiable

---

[17] There are at least five different versions of the speech, all written many years after the fact. See: "Medieval Sourcebook: Urban II (1088-1099): Speech at the Council of Clermont, 1095, Five versions of the Speech" compiled by Paul Halsall. Robert the Monk's version contains this passage about Jerusalem: "This royal city, therefore, situated at the centre of the world, is held captive by His enemies, and is in subjection to those who do not know God, to the worship of the heathens. She seeks therefore and desires to be liberated, and does not cease to implore you to come to her aid" (par. 4). Robert the Monk also specifically mentions the torments Christians are allegedly being subjected to, including "the abominable rape of the women" (par. 2).

condition of their marriage to their Saracen lover. On the other hand, is the Christian damsel who is sold into slavery, abducted, blackmailed, or otherwise forcibly married to a heathen king. This woman is morally tasked with converting the pagans around her to the Christian cause through her superior virtue and beauty, or through performing or facilitating divine miracles like the unnamed princess of Tars. The Christian damsel, through her patience and suffering, takes on some overtones of the hagiography. If she is forced to convert from Christianity, the conversion is for the public eye only. She practices her own faith in secret and waits for the right time to return to the Christian fold with her husband, children, and often her whole adopted nation in tow.

Romance heroines on both sides of the East/West divide have the quality of pragmatism, especially religious pragmatism, in common. It is not their job to die for their faith. Their job is to convert souls to Christianity, even if that means playing a political long game. The Christian heroines do this by seducing their kings (and by default, their new countries) away from their pagan ways. The Saracen princess seduces the Christian knight-hero and brings him wealth, land, kingship, and the possibility of future Christian subjects as a dowry. The seduction of the Saracen princess does not usually yield the wholesale conversion of a nation, at least not immediately, but there is at least one notable exception. Towards the end of *Bevis of Hampton*, Bevis and Josian's son Guy is named the heir to the kingdom of Ermony.[18] Upon his ascension, Guy and Bevis convert the Saracen nation:

> þanne sire Beues and sire Gii
> Al þe londe of Ermony
> Hii made Cristen wiþ dent of swerd,
> ӡong and elde, lewed and lered. (3841-44)

---

[18] Armenia

Ermony is Josian's ancestral home, and it was there in her father's court that Bevis was raised amongst Saracens. Her own conversion to Christianity remained a small matter between the lovers because she abandoned her faith and people to be with Bevis, who was more interested in retaking the English land rightfully his. Yet, on her father's death, Josian's Christian-knight son becomes a king and Christianizes the country. In this instance, Josian blurs the line between the Saracen and Christian heroines. She originally converted for the love of a Christian knight, but she then raised her sons to be Christian knights. Like the Christian damsels, her own country is ultimately converted through her influence, after all.

In this chapter, I will examine three romance heroines as instruments of colonialism through conversion. I shall focus on two fiery Saracen princesses: Josian of *Bevis of Hampton* and Floripas of *Firumbras;* and the nameless Christian princess who facilitates the conversion of an entire nation in the *King of Tars*.

The Saracen Princess and Fantasy

As mentioned above, the typical Saracen princess might not facilitate the wholesale conversion of her country, but she does serve as an important symbol of Western Europe's dreams of colonialism. Unlike her Christian sisters, the Saracen princess is memorable for her spirited temperament, courage, and forwardness in her desire for the Christian knight of her choosing. Whereas Christian damsels need to be wooed, Saracen princesses actively pursue the Christian knights they love, even going so far as to betray their families and religion to marry their knight, as Josian does with Bevis (*Bevis* 1105-32). In *Empire of Magic*, Geraldine Heng writes,

> Melaz, Fatima, Bramimonde, Orable, Floripas, and their Saracen sisters tend to figure conversion as *individual* occurrences, the behavior of memorable royal women who are valued as much for their quirky spunkiness or their fantasized excess of libido, as for their availability as cultural signs that witness, at the highest level, the superiority

> of the Christian religion. Significantly, the narratives within which these quixotic Oriental women appear do not depict the nation of Islam converting en masse because of the women's agency as figures of conversion. To be sure, any conversion by a queen or princess to the religion of the conquerors attests a colonizing impetus at work in representation, but the historical epoch's principle preoccupations write that colonization as a private love story mostly involving the important, high-level individuals who are the usual actors in elite cultural fantasy. (186)

The Saracen princess is a textual instrument of the power of colonialism because by "conquering" her through seduction, the Christian knight symbolically conquers the territory and people she represents. It is not enough for the Christian heroes to win battles and territory during their crusade, they must also win the powerful women who are native to the region. The act of a beautiful Saracen princess choosing an invading knight over the suitors of her own race and religion is imagined in romance as a symbolic acknowledgement of the cultural and religious superiority—even righteousness—of the Christian cause.

Furthermore, marrying the Saracen princess and gaining her country is an attractive fantasy in terms of upward mobility. During the eleventh century in Europe, the population grew unmanageable, particularly at the aristocratic level. In short, there were too many younger sons and not enough land, titles, or income to go around. One of the impetuses of the First Crusade, according to H. E. J. Cowdrey, was that the aristocracy of Europe was on the verge of ripping itself apart over a lack of assets and needed to vent their energies and greed elsewhere: "the surpluses of male offspring of the military classes came under pressure to seek new outlets for their martial and predatory energies at a distance from their places of birth" (14). Furthermore, these concerns are obliquely referred to in the various versions of Urban II's Council of Clermont speech, wherein he exhorts the nobility of Europe to stop petty warfare amongst each other and turn their collective attentions to crusading. Balderic of Dol's version includes the following admonishment: "You, girt about with the badge of knighthood, are arrogant with great pride; you rage against your brothers and cut each other in pieces. This is not the (true) soldiery of Christ" (par. 4). Fulcher of Chartres's version complains about European lawlessness: "It is so bad in some of your provinces, I am told, and you are so weak in administration of justice, that one can hardly go along the road by day or night without being attacked by robbers; and whether at home or abroad one is in danger of being despoiled either by force or fraud" (par. 2). Prior to the First Crusade, Europe's population of aristocracy was growing too large for its resources, and the resulting strife and lawlessness threatened social order. In this environment, the romance fantasy of going on crusade to foreign lands, catching the eye of a foreign princess, and gaining the wealth, prestige, and acclaim denied to the plethora of knights and younger sons in Europe would be attractive. The Saracen princess is the embodiment of the ultimate upward mobility fantasy: the rich, gorgeous woman who enables her knightly lover to become a king.

Also attractive to a Western European audience of medieval romance is the Saracen princess herself—and her attractiveness might not be simply limited to the romance's male audience. The Saracen princess may well grab the attention of her female audience as well because there are few developed female characters in epic and romance. Lynn Tarte Ramey explains, "the Saracen women provide the only really inviting point of entrance for a female in the epic audience. A female listener would have to choose whether to identify with the Saracen women, though they are opposed to the French, or no woman at all, due to the lack of interesting French protagonists" (135). Although Ramey specifically discusses medieval French epic in the essay, the point stands for medieval English romance. Female listeners of the crusade romances have more limited options of representation in these texts, leaving women in the unenviable position of identifying with the male protagonists, the Christian women characters who are little more than prizes to be won or who have very small parts in the story, or the tempestuous Saracen woman. The Saracen princess, although she may be Other, is also the closest thing to a medieval action heroine: intelligent, beautiful, violent, mysterious, and desiring/desirable.

The audience identification with the Saracen princess is often strengthened by her physical appearance. In her excellent study of Saracen women in French epics, *Sheba's Daughters*, Jacqueline de Weever examines the tangled ways race, ethnicity, and imperialism are written onto the bodies of female Saracen characters. One way that medieval poets contended with difficult female Saracen characters involved erasing or enhancing their racial or ethnic realities; in other words, the convertible female Saracen is already white, whereas the Saracen women who are unwilling to convert or submit to Western Christianity are often described as black or are even written as giants. Weever writes, "All heroines have a fixed portrait, invariably that of a Frankish woman in French poems. Conversely, the Saracen princess who challenges the Franks is a wild black woman. The portraits of the Saracen princesses become extensions of the binary oppositions of the culture of the time, the foundations of which are Latin Christian/Oriental pagan, white/black, orthodoxy/heterodoxy, truth/error" (xvii). In medieval epic and romance, the ideal Saracen woman has the wealth and glamour of the East, even while she appears Western: "the Easterner must not look like an Easterner, while at the same time she represents the wealth of the East, a desirable product the West hankers after" (Weever 29). The portrait of the white Saracen is an attempt to soothe the anxieties of miscegenation that she embodies. Jeffrey Jerome Cohen writes, "Such women convert eagerly to Christianity, and their embrace of their new religion is more a declaration of what they always were (white—that is, Christian—before the fact) than a true conversion from one state to another" (121). Although, whiteness aside, how ideologically soothing a Western audience would ultimately find the Saracen princess is lost to history. After all, she behaves in many ways most audiences, especially a Western audience, would find suspicious. She betrays her family and people, engages in violence, sexually desires the hero and actively woos him.

    The Saracen princess exists in a liminal space where different possibilities can play out in terms of race and religion: she is ethnically and religiously a Saracen, yet she converts to Christianity and physically appears indistinguishable from her European sisters. Ultimately, she becomes neither: she has a public track record of untrustworthiness toward her Saracen brethren, and when she converts, it is for the love of a man instead of any genuine proven feeling for a new religion. She behaves the untrustworthy villain but remains a friend to her Christian lover and his confederates, at least until she is betrayed. Another way of thinking of the Saracen princess is as the medieval version of the Bond Girl: beautiful, mysterious, treacherous, competent, ethnically stereotyped, and sexually forward with the hero. The Saracen princess is neither completely the Western 'us' or the Eastern 'them' but an uneasy male fantasy of power, where colonialism is synonymous with seduction.

    Still, there is another way to ameliorate the anxieties of the threatening and foreign Other that the Saracen princess represents: by casting her in the familiar mold of the foreign queen. An English audience would understand the role of the Saracen princess as a foreign queen in the romance because so many of their historical queens—and often their most infamous queens—were foreign-born and tasked with diplomacy both internationally and within the English court. In *Saracens and the Making of English Identity*, Siobhain Bly Calkin writes,

> Ultimately, by representing both the realm and foreign threats to it, the queen suggests the continuity of the realm in the face of all events, even as her very origins are a constant reminder of the realm's vulnerability as an entity. She embodies both the group's identity and threats to that identity simultaneously. The foreign queen thus finds herself at the meeting point of various components of a polity's self-conception. (66)

The Saracen princess is reminiscent of the foreign queen because she inhabits the liminal space of the outsider located at the very heart of the royal court. She represents both the threatening foreign Other, as well as the culture and religion she has newly adopted by marriage and conversion. Furthermore, the foreign queen not only brings an economic advantage to the marriage, but she is also responsible for important peacemaking and diplomatic functions at home and abroad: "Her prestige reinforces [her husband's] position at home by manifesting publicly his connections to royalty in the world at large. Her links to other powers allow her to serve as mediator between him and foreign powers, and thus facilitate his geopolitical interests" (Calkin 65). In other words, the foreign queen is integral to international relations between powers and bolsters her king's own international importance (and by extension, his country's own standing) with hers. Still, the connection between the Saracen princess and the role of the foreign queen is not completely safe. Historically speaking, blatant and public mutiny of foreign royal wife against her English husband, queen against king, was rare but not unprecedented. Foreign queens bring resources and alliances to her union, but if her loyalty wavers she may also use those connections to rebel. Infamously, the lovely and treacherous Eleanor of Aquitaine took sides with her sons against their father, Henry II, and spent over a decade under house arrest because of it in the mid-twelfth century. Just as well known is the example of Isabella, wife of Edward II, who gained the sobriquet the "She-Wolf of France" for her role in the usurpation of the throne from her husband the king in the early fourteenth century. Granted, she did not wrest the throne away and give it to a foreign power, but gave it to her teenage son, Edward III and continued ruling the country in his stead until he was old enough to rebel against her. Regardless, the actions of these foreign queens resulted in a fair amount of internal strife for England (and to some extent, France as well) and prove that while a foreign queen may be a boon for her new country and court, she also has the influence to undermine its stability.

There is yet a third way that the Saracen princess might ultimately soothe fears of the Western audience: romantic love. The Christian damsels might be married forcibly to their Saracen husbands and exhibit no warm feelings towards them, but the crusade romances make a point of the Saracen heroine's amorous attachment to her lover. She chooses him above all other suitors who cast themselves at her feet, begging for notice, or who skip the wooing pleasantries altogether and simply kidnap her with the intent to forcibly marry her or make her his mistress, which is what happens between Josian and the Earl Miles.[19] He first tries to make her his mistress, which she refuses and buys time by suggesting he marry her properly:

> Nought, thigh I scholde lese me lif,
> Boute ich were thee wedded wif;
> Yif eni man me scholde wedde.
> Thanne mot ich go with him to bedde. (3163-66)

Josian rejects all suitors who are not Bevis, and in Miles's case, his refusal to take no for an answer leads her to murder him in self-defense on their wedding night (3220-24). Even though she convinced Miles to marry her, she will not betray Bevis. The romances make clear that everything the Saracen princess does—betrayal, murder, scheming plots—are all

---

[19] This repeatedly happens to Josian. She is married to King Yvor against her wishes (1455-60), is abducted by Miles (3161-78), and again abducted by Ascopard and returned to her original husband Yvor who does not want her anymore since she made herself look ugly with herbs (3645-3700).

done out of love and loyalty to her knight. She *is* ostensibly a threat, but often presented as more a threat to her own people rather than the crusaders.

Floripas the Courteous

For this work, I am using the 1935 EETS edition of *Firumbras*, edited from the Fillingham MS by Mary Isabelle O'Sullivan. The romance is one of the Middle English Charlemagne romances. There are a few variants on the tale, but they all originate from a late twelfth-century *chanson de geste* called *Fierabras*. According to Leila Norako of the University of Rochester Crusades Project, the Firumbras Group includes the romances of *Sir Firumbras*, *The Sowdon of Babylon*, and *Charles the Grete*. O'Sullivan's edition includes both items in the Fillingham MS,[20] *Firumbras* and *Otuel and Roland*. The MS itself is dated from the second half of the fifteenth century, although *Firumbras* was probably composed during the late fourteenth century (Database of Middle English Romance).

The romance follows the adventures of a brother-sister pair of Saracens who are the children of the Sultan Balam. Firumbras has already converted to Christianity and defected to Charlemagne's side and his sister, Floripas, has fallen in love with the knight Guy of Burgundy and has also abandoned her father to join the crusaders. In *English Medieval Romance*, W. R. J. Barron briefly examines the variants, and of the Fillingham manuscript he writes, "Though equally fascinated by action [as the other variants], its author outlines the incidents with clarity and economy, setting scenes with a minimum of descriptive detail, allowing the characters to speak for themselves in a way which reveals them as youthful, impulsive, full of zest for life, largely independent of codes and conventions" (103). The romance is more tightly and succinctly written than the other versions of the romance group,

---

[20] Also known as the London, British Library, MS Additional 37492

and the characters themselves are bright and vivacious, including Floripas, who is irrepressible. Although there are several variants of the tale, I will focus only on this version of *Firumbras* and the way the romance portrays Floripas. Since the romance is incomplete, we miss out on some of the actions that the Floripas in the alternate versions carries out, namely at least two murders. Also, as Barron notes above, the romance is tightly written. Many extraneous details, including physical details of appearance, are missing. For example, the poet does not describe Floripas except in the vaguest details. Instead of a catalogue of Floripas's beauty—perhaps that existed in the missing leaves of the MS—we get a brief and half-hearted sketch of Floripas looking out of her tower window while awaiting news of Guy's impending rescue from the Saracens: "Mayde floryp loked out at the toun / So red as any rose was here colour" (691-2). This description does not give much away, except that she has a rosy complexion. Her value in the romance does not center on her physical beauty but in her wit and courtesy.

In fact, courtesy seems to be the quality that defines Floripas the most since the poet keeps attaching it to her name and reputation. In line 700, Guy hears Floripas celebrating his rescue and is inspired to fight harder in her honor when he hears her rejoice in his freedom: "The mayde of here wordis ys ful curtays. / By swete god of heuene, now y wyl asay, / Y wyl for here loue a lyte strokes paye!" (700-2). Guy and Floripas are acting their parts in the courtly love tradition: Floripas is the inspiration and observer of Guy's battle prowess, and he does his best to impress her and win worship with his fighting skills. Regardless of her treachery to her own people and her willingness to threaten Roland and the Franks to get what she wants, beyond her own physical beauty, and although she is Saracen, Floripas is above all a lady of courtesy. The descriptor appears again later: "floryp the curtays that ys so fayre a may" (1205). According to the Middle English Dictionary, cŏurteis as an adjective refers to a host of behaviors:

> 1(a) Of persons: courtly or refined in manners; well-bred, urbane; polite, courteous; considerate, kind; ...
> 2. Gracious, benevolent, generous, merciful ...
> 3. Respectful, deferential, meek" (*MED* n.pag.).

No one would accuse Floripas of being meek, but she consistently displays courtesy and a courtliness to rival any Frankish princess to the Franks under her care because she loves Guy and respects his comrades. Although she is not a Christian until her conversion at the end of the romance, Floripas is admired by the Frankish warriors who have accepted her presence among them, even as her father curses the hour of her birth: "'wrotherhayle,' sayd Balam, 'that tyme that sche was borne!'" (807). Both of Balam's children have abandoned him; but although Firumbras is now fighting for the Franks, it is Floripas that seems to frustrate Balam the most because it is through her protection that the Franks have withstood war and siege. Both Firumbras and Floripas have both accepted and found reciprocal acceptance in their new communities.

Floripas shows her courtesy and acceptance of the Franks by being accommodating to their beliefs and keeping the peace. She does not get agitated by religious difference the way that they do. Instead, she views religion pragmatically as a means to an end. As mentioned above, Saracen princesses tend to convert for love of a man, more than out of any love of a god or religion. When conditions in the besieged tower are dire because of a lack of food, she suggests praying to her gods (233-38). The Franks are appalled, and when she takes them to the temple[21] of stone idols, the Franks destroy them and tell her to leave off her false ways

---

[21] The word the text uses to describe the room is "synagog" (246). In this detail, the poet conflates the Islamic mosque with the Jewish synagogue.

(264-75). Far from being offended, Floripas takes the destruction of her gods in stride, saying to Roland:

> "syr," sche seyde, "þat y se and so thenketh me:
> Thay ne be but metal and stynkke as an hounde:
> I be-take hem to be þe deuyl þat lyȝth in helle y-bounde.
> But pray we to god þat ys in mageste,
> Þat y-bore was of a mayde in clene virginite;
> That Charlys mote come sonewith hys chyualrye." (276-81)

As far as Floripas is concerned, if praying to her gods scandalizes the Franks, then they can all pray to the Christian god instead, just so long as someone prays to some higher power for salvation. She gamely admits to the Franks that her gods are just empty images and even adds an insult of her own, that the images stink like a hound (277) for emphasis. If for the Saracen princess conversion is just the price of admission to marrying her Christian lover, then Floripas will be no exception to that rule; she recognizes her need to integrate into the Frankish community completely if she wants to marry one of their own.

However, there is a catch to her willingness to help the Franks and support their cause for the love of a man, because when Guy of Burgundy is no longer there, she considers herself under no obligation to continue being cooperative in their plans. Unlike her brother Firumbras, who converts and joins Charlemagne allegedly out of genuine religious feeling, Floripas's helpfulness is conditional. Her ferocity and wartime stratagems, thus far turned on her own father and his troops, could just as easily be brought to bear on the Franks and they are aware of it. Upon hearing of Guy's capture, she flies into a rage and says,

> By that ylke lord that tholed woundes fiue,
> ȝow ne schal waraunt no man on lyue!
> But ȝe feche a-ȝen my lord that ȝe haue lore, —
> To wrotherhayl the tyme that euer ȝe ware y-bore! —
> I schal ȝelde the tour with-Inne the thrydde day
> And ȝe to be don to deth the foulyst that man may. (482-7)

If they do not rescue Guy, she will not only betray the remaining Franks by yielding the besieged tower to her father and his army, but she will make sure that the Franks—and Roland in particular—will be executed in as horrible a manner as can be devised. There are a couple specific points of interest about this passage. First, conscious of her audience, this still-unconverted Saracen princess swears an oath by Christ ("that ylke lord that tholed woundes fiue") instead of Saracen gods to impress on them the weight of her threat. Driving that point home, she gives a deadline of three days: if they cannot return her lord to her, then on the third day she will hand them and the tower over to the Saracens with nary a moment of regret. The threat has threads of Christ's resurrection woven into it; if Guy is not "resurrected" within three days, her cooperation ceases and her campaign begins.

Roland, famed and brave hero of many a *chanson de geste* and romance, is thoroughly unnerved by her mercenary attitude and takes seriously her promise to send them all into captivity and grisly execution: "Tho by-gan Roulond hys hert to quake / ffor hys fellow Gy and that maydenes sake" (488-9). Roland knows that Guy's fate will determine the fate of the Franks, and if Guy is killed before can be rescued, Floripas will keep her word and hand them over to the Saracens. By the same token, if Guy is rescued and brought back to Floripas alive, the Franks will also survive with Floripas's continued protection. It is a testament to the Franks' regard for Floripas that no one questions her authority or chastises her. Accordingly, Roland promises to bring Guy back by the end of the next day instead (495). Floripas is not quite appeased, but responds icily:

> By that ylke oth that thou hast sworne & ply3t,
> But thow holde me couenaunt to-morwe or hit be ny3t,
>
> Ne schal neuer kyng charlys, ne none of hys lynage
> Come in thys toure, ne none of hys baronage! (496-99)

The implications are grim for the tower's current inhabitants. Guy is the price of her assistance. On the one hand, this makes sense—she holds them responsible for abandoning Guy in the field to be captured and unless they rectify their mistake, she will punish them all. On the other hand, this passage highlights her lack of political loyalty to either Saracens or Franks, even as it highlights her personal loyalty to Guy. Best case scenario, the Saracens keep Guy as a captive, and presumably she can negotiate for him by yielding the tower to the Saracens and thus be able to rescue or save Guy herself by being able to reintegrate herself as a Saracen. Worst case scenario, the Saracens execute Guy—which is Balam's first impulse when he finds out the knight in his possession is his troublesome daughter's lover (520). If Guy dies, Floripas seems to intend to cause the most chaos she can manage by exacting revenge on the community immediately within reach: the Franks. In either case, it is not clear how the Saracens themselves would deal with Floripas's shifting loyalties. Happily, Floripas does not have to follow through on her threats because Guy is rescued from death and she is overjoyed (694-99).

A final point of interest regarding Floripas is her conversion scene because it is presented as a stark contrast to the failed conversion of her father, Balam. Balam is offered conversion three times. Floripas's brother Firumbras asks Charlemagne to offer the sultan terms of surrender and conversion (1451-64), a request the Frankish king readily grants on behalf of his newest knight (1670). Later, Firumbras begs his father to take conversion (1681-85) and Balam appears to relent, until the bishop takes him to the fountain. The sultan attacks the bishop and although Firumbras begs for him one more time, Balam outright refuses conversion for the third time and is immediately beheaded (1685-1718). Floripas has no such moments of vacillation. Charlemagne will not allow her to marry Guy of Burgundy until she converts to Christianity. Floripas, ever pragmatic, sees a public and immediate opportunity for her conversion and disrobes for her baptism:

> Whenne floryp that herde, nolde sche not slake
> That Cristendom sche wolde anone at the funston take.
> She kest of her Clothys, all folke a-forne,
> And stode ther naked as sche was borne.
> The good byschope that was of grete pryse
> Crystenede the mayde & dude the seruise.
> Tho for-soke floryp Mahoun and hys lay,
> Toke sche to here ihesu to serue both ny3t & day. (1763-40)

This scene is jarring. One moment, Floripas sees her own father beheaded, and in the next moment, she takes off her clothes and demands immediate baptism: "nolde sche not slake / That Cristendom sche wolde anone at the funston take" very clearly indicates that Floripas will not be put off even a moment. She has fought a war and betrayed both her family and people to get the man she wants, so she is not going to let a little thing like religion get in her way for another moment. She has already repudiated her own gods in front of the Frankish heroes and has begun to use references to Christianity in her speech patterns. Baptism just makes official what she has demonstrated throughout the romance.

There is also an element of voyeurism and exoticism in this passage—it is difficult to imagine a demure Christian damsel stripping in public, let alone in front of a group of men including her brother, a king, a bishop, her lover, her father's corpse, and their entire retinue. Floripas is, until the very last moment of her heathenism, a Saracen princess defiant of convention. Furthermore, while stripping down is rare for an adult baptism, the phrase "naked as sche was borne" strongly implies a spiritual rebirth. Like the sultan in *The King of Tars*, Floripas sheds her old identity with her clothes and steps into the baptismal fount. Floripas's Saracen identity is destroyed in the fount, and she emerges from baptism as a new Christian. Her conversion is toward the end of the romance, and she only appears once more when she gifts Charlemagne with the holy relics from the tower (1768-74). She once again demonstrates her courtesy, because although Charles only asked to see the relics before he returns for France, "Sche made a Ryche presaunt to Charlys the kynge" (1774) of all the relics that had been in her keeping. This last detail gives her character an unexpected twist because we have seen her disregard for her own gods when she was a Saracen, but she has quietly kept some of the most precious Christian relics safe throughout the entire story. Our last glimpse of Floripas as a Christian woman is also a glimpse of her as a guardian of the faith who then entrusts the relics to Charles.

Floripas shares many similarities with other Saracen princesses, including the fierce and manipulative Josian. Floripas is vivacious, intelligent, ambitious, and proves herself a capable leader and strategist throughout the entire romance. Also, so long as she has Guy at her side, she is willing to guard the Franks under her protection. Josian is cut from much the same cloth and joins the ranks of accomplished romance women, either Saracen or Christian, with her own daring and practical knowledge of medicine and minstrelsy.

Josian, the Distressing Damsel

For this work, I am using the version found in *Four Romances of England: King Horn, Havelok the Dane, Bevis of Hampton, and Athelston*, edited by Ronald B. Herzman, Graham Drake, and Eve Salisbury. The romance exists in six different English manuscripts and descends from the Anglo-Norman *Boeve*. Scholarship on the romance often focuses on the way the romance treats identity. In *Bevis of Hampton* (*Bevis*), identity is fundamentally unstable and multifaceted in terms of nationality, family, religion, and gender. In "Defining Christian Knighthood in a Saracen World," Siobhan Bly Calkin examines multiple versions of the romance to trace the way *Bevis* either changes or remains the same to reflect the ideal

Christian knighthood of each version's respective times (144). Knighthood is only one facet of identity presented in the romance; gender is also a concern. In Corinne Saunder's essay "Gender, Virtue and Wisdom in *Sir Bevis of Hampton*," she argues that Josian complicates gender stereotypes:

> Josian both is and is not the romance lady familiar from French romance: while she is defined by courtly virtues and qualities, including her appearance, she fits the more active 'wooing woman' type found in Anglo-Norman romance and chanson de geste. She also recalls the protagonists of legends of holy women, empowered through virginity and chastity. Josian's Christian virtue, however, is interwoven with her 'otherness', her Saracen origin, which plays and important role in rendering acceptable her remarkable powers of medicine, healing and protection, as well as her proactiveness in wooing and in preserving her chastity. She is further elaborated through her difference from Bevis's mother ... The portrayals of Bevis and Josian depend upon the elaboration of their individual virtue and wisdom as much as upon the expected romance roles of knight and lady in situations of love and war. (162-63).

Because *Bevis* is fundamentally rooted in questions about national, religious, and personal identity, both the hero and heroine have the unenviable task of determining who they are to each other and how they fit into Saracen and Christian societies. Josian's Saracen-ness allows her more freedom in her actions (e.g. her active wooing of Bevis, and defensive preservation of her virginity and later chastity) because she might be on her way to becoming Christian, but her conversion is also a journey where she must learn her new place in the Christian world order. The romance examines identity as both inherent and as a product of environment and desire: Bevis is a Christian who grows up amongst Saracens and retains little actual knowledge of his own religion from his early childhood. His goal to retake his inheritance in England is stymied by the fact that Bevis no longer quite belongs in England, nor does his converted-Saracen princess wife, Josian. While Bevis struggles with his own dual identities of English-Christian and Christian-raised-by-Saracens, my interest is in the way Josian navigates and manipulates her own identity primarily to keep Bevis. Like

Floripas, Josian converts to Christianity for love of a man, not out of any special interest in Christianity.

If the pragmatic Floripas functions within her own text as an embodiment of generic conversion anxieties attached to the Saracen princess type, Josian's character is comparatively worrying to the Christian audience. From the beginning, Josian proves herself highly intelligent, adaptable, loyal to her lover, and a brilliant stateswoman, adept at maneuvering the men in her life to her best advantage and just as adept at murdering them when they do not cooperate or when they threaten her virtue. The Earl Miles, for instance, kidnaps and tries to seduce her, but Josian feigns maidenly shyness to get him to dismiss the servants and lock the bedroom door (3193-3213), enabling her to ambush him:

> Josian bethoughte on highing,
> On a towaile she made knotte riding,
> Aboute his nekke she hit threw
> And on the raile tre she drew;
> Be the nekke she hath him up tight
> And let him so ride al the night.
> Josian lai in hire bed (3219-3225)

Josian takes the opportunity that a moment of privacy affords her and murders Miles by strangling him. Then she lays down in the bed, knowing full well in the morning that she would be discovered and punished for it. Yet, her resolve remains firm and her loyalty remains entirely with the absent Bevis. When questioned the next morning about why she killed Miles, she says,

> Yerstendai he me wedded with wrong
> And tonight ichave him honge.
> Doth be me al youre wille,
> Schel he never eft wimman spille! (3253-3256)

Josian's argument is primarily self-defense, and the defense of women he might try to prey on in the future. The earl behaved dishonorably toward her ("wedded with wrong") since she was already married of her own free will to Bevis, and she asserts that she is within her rights to retaliate. The episode is only one of a few when Josian is menaced by men who want to abduct/marry her (see footnote 19), but it illustrates her own sense of agency and the lengths she is willing to go to protect herself. For the entire seven years she was married to King Yvor, she wore a magic ring to protect her virginity: "While ichave on that ilche ring, / To me schel no man have welling" (1471-72). When Bevis questions her on her virginity, she tells him that he can test her word by asking any of her maids, and if that is not enough for him: "Send me aghen to me fon / Al naked in me smok alon!" (2205-06). This detail comes back in the aftermath of Miles's murder: Bevis narrowly rescues Josian from being publicly burnt at the stake: "In hire smok she stod naked / Thar the fur was imaked" (3289-90). Josian's loyalty to Bevis is complete, and she is willing to murder and die for it.

Josian has long been an interest of scholars because her nature in the romance is complicated in terms of power dynamics between her and Bevis. Myra Seaman calls Josian the "shadow hero" of the romance because she upsets the conventions of romance heroine behavior by behaving more like the active hero than a passive heroine (56). In "A Good Woman is Hard to Find," Bonnie J. Erwin argues that Josian troubles gender and power dynamics in *Bevis* not by her refusal to submit to Bevis, but instead by very consciously submitting on her own conditions rather than his:

> Josian's conversion is more unsettling than the paradigm [of performing acts of queenly intercession] allows because she not only claims a position of power for herself as Calkin notes, but also draws attention to how much Bevis's own power is contingent upon her willingness to grant it. Josian constructs herself as an object in submitting to Bevis; however, she is an object of utmost importance, the possession of which is crucial to the performance of knighthood. (378)

In other words, Josian is troubling for Bevis precisely because Bevis's own power and prestige as a knight is granted, in part, by her. He does not have the power to command her submission to him or to his god; such power must be and is consciously surrendered by Josian. This complicates the power dynamics; he cannot take what is not freely given, and the power to consent is hers. Furthermore, his prowess as a knight is based not only on his service to his lord, but also in being devoted to a lady (Erwin 377). In effect, Bevis needs Josian far more than she needs him. Moreover, Erwin draws from Homi Bhabha's ideas about the "mimic man"[22] and colonialism, calling Josian a "mimic woman" who is "not quite" Christian even though she converts (371). Josian destabilizes power in the text by revealing the gendered underpinnings of such power. Erwin argues that,

> Josian ... creates instability not only because of her identity as a convert, but also because of her intransigent gender difference. The text's treatment of Josian as a mimic woman reveals that the Christian way of life is sustained by women's compliance with the patriarchal order—an order that requires them to serve as tools for reproducing noble lineage, as well as admirers who validate chivalric masculinity. (371-2)

In other words, Josian does not submit to Bevis naturally, unthinkingly, or because it never occurs to her to be anything other than submissive. On the contrary, Christianity and its prescribed gender roles are not paradigms she has experience with: "Boute of Cristene lawe she kouthe naught" (*Bevis* 526). Instead, she consciously shapes her own identity to fit into the new gendered role Christianity demands from her, which only reveals the artificiality inherent in the Christian power structures—and in gender power structures. Seaman argues that, "Her active disavowal of the stereotypical qualities of femininity questions the presumably natural connection between those qualities and individual female bodies. Further, her conscious performance at times of those characteristics demonstrates that they are not

---

[22] In his book, *The Location of Culture*, Homi Bhabha considers mimicry as a method of colonialism that normalizes the colonial state: "colonial mimicry is the desire for a reformed, recognizable Other, as a subject of a difference that is almost the same but not quite" (122). Similarly, the mimic man or woman exists in a liminal space between the colonizers and the colonized, and who essentially becomes a translator between the two states. He or she has the education, tastes, and manners of the colonizers, but resembles the colonized and in the end, is neither completely one or the other (125).

innate since they can be taken up—and laid aside—by individuals" (69). Josian proves that submission is not actually a natural state for women, but a choice, just as she has a choice to convert to Christianity when Bevis rejects her love: "ich wile right now to mede / Min false godes al forsake / And Christendom for thee love take!" (1194-96). She converts to make her peace with him and gain his love, not out of any love of Christianity, which she knows little about.

To be fair, Bevis himself knows little about Christianity and it is a Saracen knight who, paradoxically, knows more about Christianity than the allegedly Christian knight. While Bevis is out riding with fifteen Saracens, one of them asks him if he knows what day it is, and Bevis replies that he does not and is informed that it is Christmas day (591-601). The Saracen helpfully points out not only the day, but the reason Christians celebrate it, and encourages Bevis to do so:

> The Sarasin beheld and lough.
> "This dai," a saide, "I knowe wel inough.
> This is the ferst dai of Youl,
> Thee God was boren withouten doul;
> For thi men maken ther mor blisse
> Than men do her in hethenesse.
> Anour thee God, so I schel myne,
> Both Mahoun and Apolyn!" (599-606)

The interesting thing about this passage is that the Saracen explains the importance of Christmas (even if he calls it Yule, which has Germanic and Anglo-Saxon pagan connotations) by mentioning that it is the day that Christ was born. He excuses Bevis from having known it because Bevis lives "in hethenesse" where the day is not celebrated as much—but the implication of lines 603-4 is that the holiday is known and celebrated at least a little even in their land, and that Bevis should have at least marked it. This exchange is not as unusual as one might first think. In her fascinating study of Christian, Jewish, and Muslim women in medieval Iberia, María Jesús Fuente writes that women of the different faiths often respected the various foodways and customs of their neighbors, helped each other with childbirth and childcare, and would largely ignore religious authorities who called for segregation by hosting parties and even visiting each other's places of worship (328-329). She notes that although the women had a significant amount of interaction with each other, "contact did not lead to assimilation" (328). Each group maintained their own boundaries, while still understanding those of their neighbors. In this light, the Saracen knight makes more sense. He tells Bevis he should "Anour thee God" on this special day, and espouses an idea of religious tolerance, that each of them should worship their own gods. Practical history aside, this is a fascinating line—and a shocking one to find in a medieval English romance. "Anour thee God, and so I schele myne" is a paraphrase of chapter 109 of the Quran[23] which is short and says this:

> Say, "O disbelievers,
> I do not worship what you worship.
> Nor are you worshippers of what I worship.
> Nor will I be a worshipper of what you worship.
> Nor will you be worshippers of what I worship.
> For you is your religion, and for me is my religion." (Quran 109: 1-6)

This line appearing in this romance may well be a coincidence. After all, we do not know the author(s) of the romance, or their backgrounds or education. However, it is entirely possible that the poet might have had some textual knowledge or encounters with a Latinate translation of the Quran.

Considering that the Quran was read and studied (if only so that Christian scholars could write polemics about it), it is entirely possible—even likely—that the writer of *Bevis*

---

[23] Thanks again to Dylan Charpentier for his assistance with Muslim theology and resources. Unfortunately, I do not have access to a medieval Quran in translation, so I have had to make do with a more modern Arabic-English facing-page translation.

had at least a passing encounter with the Quran. After all, while it is true that wild misconceptions about Islam found their way into mainstream and popular texts (such as the enduring ideas that Saracens were idolators and polytheists as illustrated in the reference to Mahoun and Apolyn being gods), the crusades necessitated textual engagement, a "know thy enemy" way of thinking, as Muzaffar Iqbal puts it (91). The variety of anti-Muslim polemic texts of the twelfth century and beyond needed something concrete to argue against in their debates. Iqbal points at Peter the Venerable as being instrumental in translations of the Quran: "He forcefully advocated the cause of studying Islam from its own sources and himself traveled to Spain in 1142, where he gathered a team of translators to produce Latin translations to a number of key Arabic texts" (91). Among the texts translated, of course, was the Quran. The Latinate Quran produced from this early translation endeavor was far from perfect and included mistakes and misinterpretations, but remained the standard for the next six centuries, and was further translated into multiple vernacular languages in the sixteenth and seventeenth centuries (92-3). Thomas E. Burman, in *Reading the Qur'ān in Latin Christendom, 1140-1560*, studies the manuscript translations of the Quran, as well as the reading practices of those who engaged with it. He argues that manuscript studies—examining the construction of the manuscripts and printed editions, the ordering and nature of the accompanying texts, the commentary and marginalia readers attached to it—may give scholars an idea of how medieval audiences engaged with the Quran (5-6). In sum, the romance's poet may well have had at least a limited engagement with both the Quran and the polemic surrounding it, but we have no concrete evidence as to the translation or how much engagement the poet had with the text.

Regardless, the entire Christmas day scene between Bevis and the Saracen knight is both unexpected and subversive because the Saracen takes the time to teach him about an important aspect of the Christian religion that Bevis should know, and then advises Bevis to do whatever Christians do on Christmas to honor their God. Presumably, he means Bevis should worship or attend a service; the lines about Christian men celebrating the holiday more than those in "hethenesse" seem to suggest that there is still a celebration in their kingdom, albeit a small one. Bevis, however, misses the well-meant point entirely and starts a fight:

> Of Cristendom yit ichave abraid,
> Ichave seie on this dai right
> Armed mani a gentil knight,
> Torneande right in the feld
> With helmes bright and mani scheld;
> And were ich alse stith in plac,
> Ase ever Gii, me fader was,
> Ich wolde for me Lordes love,
> That sit high in hevene above,
> Fight with yow everichon,
> Er than ich wolde hennes gon! (608-18)

For Bevis, his idea and associations about Christmas has nothing to do with God or religion at all. He fondly recalls the Christmas celebrations of his youth before his father was murdered, when his father held tournaments and a young Bevis could admire the "gentil" knights with their "helmes bright and mani scheld." The Saracen's "live and let live" suggestion of religious tolerance is overshadowed by Bevis's sudden existential crisis: in the space of twenty-two lines, Bevis transitions from neither knowing nor caring about the day, to boasting that he wants to fight and beat them all for God's love. Bevis's own identity is intensely conflicted—for all his refusal to convert from Christianity (560-68) he has not seemed to spend much time thinking about religion in the eight years between his arrival in King Ermin's court until his fateful Christmas day battle when he is forcibly reminded of his "true" religious identity. Bevis's idea of Christmas is wrapped up in his childish recollections of the playful violence in a celebratory tourney (which he perverts into real violence with real murderous intent), as well as the following traumas of his father's murder, his mother's traitorous adultery, and his own attempted murder and exile, not peace. Christmas and the dissolution of his family blur together and the result is explosive at that moment, but it also sheds light on the way Bevis regards Josian.

The memory of Bevis's family and his mother's betrayal of it casts a long, dark shadow on his psyche, but it also provides a standard for Josian to shine against. In "Desire, Will and Intention in *Sir Beues of Hamtoun*" Corinne Saunders writes about Josian's gendered complexity, examining Josian's juxtaposition against Bevis's adulterous mother, her extensive education, and her general competency in terms of self-preservation: "She is carefully constructed to subvert conventional medieval notions of women as naturally frail and passive and, in particular, to counteract the role of Bevis's mother. She resists too the model of the courtly lady, object of desire and trophy of battle, and though she is repeatedly threatened by enforced marriage, she never becomes the damsel in distress" (174-5). Throughout the romance, Josian is presented as valiant and competent at self-preservation, able to think around her captors. Like Floripas, Josian is usually the smartest person in the room and runs circles around her father, her unwanted husbands, and the traitorous giant Ascopard. The romance's poet points out Josian's intelligence when she is first introduced as a child, early in the romance:

> Josian that maide het,
> Hire schon wer gold upon her fet;
> So fair she was and bright of mod,
> Ase snow upon the rede blod—
> Wharto scholde that may discrive?
> Men wiste no fairer thing alive,

>So hende ne wel itaught. (519-25)

Interestingly, in this introduction the poet spends equal time discussing Josian's mental faculties as her physical characteristics. We understand that she joins the bevy of generically gorgeous white Saracen princesses ("ase snow upon the rede blod"), but her physical appearance is otherwise dismissed with the line "no fairer thing alive" (524). The rest of the description is more concerned with her intelligence; she is bright of mind, gentle, and highly educated. Josian is the trifecta of the ideal woman: beautiful, brilliant, and she even has a nice personality. Seaman makes a similar observation: "While her beauty is noted and quickly demonstrated, it is continually balanced by admiration of her mind. Not only is she bright, but she has been trained and educated as well. From this beginning her mind is praised, certainly in a way far more typical of a romance hero than heroine" (57). Furthermore, the poet's insistence on Josian's intelligence and high level of education is not mere lip-service but demonstrated throughout the text. When Bevis is grievously injured after his Christmas Day massacre,[24] Josian is the one who heals him: "riche bathes she let him make, / That withinne a lite stoned / He was bothe hol and sonde" (*Bevis* 732-34), proving that her knowledge is more than theoretical.

Josian is not only an accomplished healer but she is also a valuable courtier and she demonstrates sharp political acumen and diplomacy when she protects Bevis from her own father. The king is incensed at the loss of his men in their Christmas day battle with Bevis and wants to execute Bevis in retaliation. Josian councils her father to school his temper and reminds him that he has not yet heard Bevis's account of the altercation:

>"Sire, ich wot wel in me thought,
>That thine men ne slough he nought,
>Be Mahoun ne be Tervagaunt,

---

[24] Beves shows King Ermin his "Fourti grete, grisli wounde" (724).

> Boute hit were himself defendaunt!
> Ac, fader," she saide, "be me red,
> Er thow do Bevis to ded,
> Ich praie, sire, for love o me,
> Do bringe that child before thee!
> Whan the child, that is so bold,
> His owene tale hath itolde,
> And thow wite the soth, aplight,
> Who hath the wrong, who hath right,
> Yef him his dom, that he schel have,
> Whather thow wilt him slen or save!" (657-670)

There is a lot happening in this passage because Josian is mounting a multilayered defense of Bevis to her outraged father. First, it is immediately apparent that Josian is not a pretty, useless ornament in her father's court. She asks him to be ruled by her ("be me red") and to listen to her counsel before acting. She speaks her mind freely to her father and argues a case of self-defense for Bevis. After all, the battle was all-on-one, so it is reasonable to claim that Bevis was merely defending himself against a greater number of attackers. That he was beset by a whole group of warriors transfers the dishonor of the whole affair away from Bevis, even though he started the fight. Josian invokes the names of the Saracen gods, and asks her father to be reasonable for her love if nothing else. Lines 654-5 are particularly interesting. Josian refers to Bevis as a child twice (even though Bevis is fifteen years old, thus grown), and then uses the word "bold." The implications of these words are insidious. First, she plants the idea that if her father has Bevis summarily executed, that he will be killing a child, not a man. Second, the word "bold," when coupled with the idea that the whole reason Bevis is in trouble is because he has just killed a lot of Ermin's soldiers, has decidedly positive connotations. If Bevis is executed, all the bold and violent potential of such a ferocious knight in the king's service will die with him. In other words, Josian reframes Bevis as both an innocent and an asset. Finally, she appeals to her father's sense of justice in asking him to hear Bevis's side of the story before making any judgments.

Counseling and manipulating her father is one matter, but Josian must learn to handle Bevis differently because he has a different set of expectations for her and different ideas about what kind of woman she should be. Theoretically, Josian might be willing to give up power and autonomy to keep Bevis, but the practice is another matter. During the episode of the two lions in the cave Bevis forces her, under the threat of violence and abandonment, to become the passive damsel in distress, a role which is alien to the ever-competent Saracen princess. Her pragmatic plan to hold down one of the lions to help Bevis kill them is summarily rejected:

> Dame, forsoth, ywys,
> I might yelp of lytel prys,
> There I had a lyon quelde,
> The while a woman another helde!
> Thow shalt never umbraide me,
> When thou comest hoom to my countré;
> But thou let hem goo both twoo,
> Have good day, fro thee I go! (2413-20)

Bevis requires Josian to sit quietly to the side while he battles the lions, telling her that her interference in the battle means cheapening his victory. Bevis's concern for his honor is informed entirely by gender politics. Had Josian been a man, they could battle the lions together and each gain honor from the encounter, but because Josian is a woman, any martial help she offers must be rejected if Bevis wants to maintain his masculinity. Even her offer to passively hold back one of the lions would lead to a taint on his reputation if people find out "a woman another [lion] helde" (2416). Bevis then warns her against future infractions against their gender roles, telling her she is not to challenge his authority when they return to England. The final line is particularly interesting for a romance hero to utter, especially to his supposed beloved lady. He threatens to leave her with the lions if she interferes, and so prioritizes his own masculinity and honor over the wellbeing and safety of his lady. The threat of abandonment escalates to a threat of physical violence when she thinks he is losing the battle and she tries to hold back one of the lions anyway:

> Tho Josian gan understonde,
> That hire lord scholde ben slawe;
> Helpe him she wolde fawe.
> Anon she hent that lioun:
> Beves bad her go sitte adoun,
> And swor be God in Trinité,
> Boute she lete that lioun be,
> A wolde hire sle in that destresse
> Ase fain ase the liounesse. (2470-78)

There are a couple points of interest in this passage. First, Bevis threatens to kill Josian if she interferes again with his battle. This is hardly good romance-hero behavior. Although, technically, neither one of them is acting their romance-roles very well: Bevis, as usual, misses the point of his role of romance knight-lover entirely by failing to balance the demands of the two roles, and failing to recognize that good service to his lady actually enhances his reputation instead of sullying it; and Josian fails to live up to the stereotype of the romance-heroine by virtue of not fainting dead away of terror. Instead, she displays an unusual lack of faith in her knight when she analyzes the situation and does not trust him to win the fight without her: "Josian gan understonde, / That hire lord scholde ben slawe" (2470-71). The second item of interest in this passage is the lioness itself. Bevis already killed the lioness's mate, and the female lion is easily as vicious as the male was. Another way of considering this scene is that Bevis is fighting more than just the lions; he is also fighting Josian's gender-defying agency as well. In theory, part of Josian's journey to conversion and becoming Bevis's ideal Christian wife is letting go of her active role in their adventures. In other words, he would prefer her be less of a masculine hero and more of a feminine heroine. Bevis is willing to enforce that passiveness—he will kill her as readily as he kills the lioness if she will not comply. Her offer is merely to hold back the lioness while he slays the male lion first, but even that intervention is too emasculating for Bevis to stand. If the lioness is a mirror for Josian in terms of ferocity, defense, and loyalty to her mate, Josian is offering to rein in her own nature. This is frustrating for Bevis. He does not want surrender, he wants to thoroughly defeat his opponents.

After the dramatic events and escapes of the first half of the romance, Josian's conversion scene is anti-climactic. Josian is notably silent throughout the entire scene. For a woman who speaks her mind and takes an active hand in her own life and preservation, who is brave enough to hold onto a lion to help Bevis kill it, her silence is telling. Bevis takes the momentous occasion and makes it entirely about him. She does not introduce herself when the bishop asks Bevis who she is, and Bevis does not actually introduce her either. He says, "Sire, of hethenesse a queen, / And she wile, for me sake, / Cristendome at thee take" (2582-4). The entire passage sounds more like a brag than anything: Bevis has netted himself a heathen queen willing to convert to Christianity for him alone. As above, I mentioned that Saracen princesses do not usually convert for love of God or religion, but instead they convert so they can keep and marry their Christian-knight lover. The audience knows her motivation to convert is for love of Bevis instead of God and treats it as something of an open secret, but Bevis, with his typical blundering touch, points this out explicitly. Josian's silence does not dispute him, and the bishop does not ask any questions. This is interesting; as mentioned above, the romance makes it clear that Josian knows little of Christianity, and neither does Bevis. However, the conversion scene (which, tellingly, directly follows the lion scene) shows that Christian gender politics are already at work: Josian goes meekly to her conversion with nary a word about it. Floripas all but jumped into the fountain and demanded to be baptized. From Josian we neither see nor hear any kind of enthusiasm or intent and she is uncharacteristically passive in her acceptance of her baptism. In this moment, Bevis's symbolic defeat of the lioness/Josian results in a tamed Saracen princess.

KT: The Princess of Tars

The fiery Saracen princesses discussed so far have converted for love of a single man, and do not usually bring their people with them. The Christian damsel (who may or may not be a princess; sometimes she is a captive or slave like Blancheflour, the heroine of *Floris and Blancheflour*) has a much bigger job than her Saracen sisters. She must convert not only her husband, but also an entire nation to her cause. Unlike the powerful Saracen women who convert for their knights, the marriages the Christian damsels are subjected to are not typically love matches. Acquiescing to such marriages fulfills a hagiographical impulse in the Christian damsel's characterization: she must patiently suffer the indignity of a pagan or heathen husband or suitor and demonstrate by her superior virtues the true religion. All this is demonstrated in *The King of Tars* (*KT*), which I break into three sections: the princess's agreement to marry the sultan and convert (albeit falsely), the episode surrounding the lump of flesh, and finally the conversion of the sultan himself.

The romance exists in three manuscripts: the Auchinleck (which is the version I analyze here[25]), the MS Vernon, and the MS Simeon. *KT* is the story of a beautiful Christian princess who chooses to wed the warmongering Sultan of Damascus to save her family and people from him. She pretends to convert and has a child by the sultan. The child is born a lump of featureless flesh and a competition between the sultan and his queen over whose god is true is settled when she has the lump baptized and it turns into a healthy son. The sultan, amazed, converts to Christianity, his skin color changes from black to white, and he unites

---

[25] Specifically, the text referenced here is Judith Perryman's 1980 edition for the Middle English Text Series.

with his father-in-law to forcibly convert his entire kingdom of Damascus to Christianity. The first part of the narrative introduces the audience to a very different breed of Christian heroine than they are accustomed to encountering. This is not a woman who suffers physical torture or temptation like a martyr for her religion. She does not convert others to her religion by demonstrating remarkable fortitude under physical duress. The princess of Tars is perhaps more like her Saracen sisters than we originally expect: she shares their intelligence and pragmatism, although she is more likely to resort to politically outmaneuvering her opponents instead of violence.

Many scholars have examined the sultan's miraculous transformation from black to white, and the romance's anxieties over racial and religious miscegenation. The transformation and the connection between identity and physical representation is well-trod territory, as Siobhan Bly Calkin, Jane Gilbert, and Anna Czarnowus have all written extensively about race, religion, and the *KT*. Alternatively, Lilian Herlands Hornstein takes a more historical approach in her essay "The Historical Background of the King of Tars." She discusses real Tartar rulers who served as "historical equivalents of the characters in the Middle English poem," as well as these rulers' fascination with Christianity, and the rumors that circulated during the thirteenth century about possible secret conversions—all things that might have influenced *KT* (408). Moreover, Andrea Hopkins reads *KT* as part of a collection of feminine romances that "demonstrate more conventional, socially acceptable feminine virtues, imply approval of decidedly secular values such as the enjoyment of high rank, wealth and status, and locate the arena for feminine virtue solidly in the sphere of the faithful wife—producing heirs, improving domestic comfort and negotiating familial relationships"

(129). Indeed, *KT* might be named for a man, but the heroine is certainly the main character and the force for change/conversion in the text.

The princess of Tars uses her gender and the Christianity's ideas of proper femininity like a weapon in the romance—she does not challenge her new husband's authority but passively submits to his wishes in public, regardless of her own feelings on the matter. In her essay "'Stille as Ston': Oriental Deformity in *The King of Tars*," Anna Czarnowus considers the princess as an agent of colonization. The romance ruminates on differences of ethnicity, race, and religion, but Czarnowus points out that "The difference between colonizer and colonized becomes opaque. Superficially colonized, the princess undertakes the colonizing mission" (468). The princess's easy public acceptance of Islam, while duplicitous, reveals the long-game of soft conversion tactics. Shokoofeh Rajabzadeh notes something similar on the dissolution of borders between the ideologies of the princess and the sultan by reflecting on the way the princess converts:

> The princess does not respond to conflict by fortifying her personal beliefs and resisting any exchange that could result in their contamination. This is what one would expect of a pious Christian woman, such as a saint. Rather, the princess compromises her outward Christian appearance and allows for an influx of new information from the sultan. As a result, she dissolves the border between them and establishes a communal space. (177)

While the princess's easy acquiescence might unnerve her Western European audience, who are used to hagiographies of saintly women and virgins who would rather go to their deaths than compromise their beliefs—even for show—the princess's job in this romance is not to die a tragic death as a martyr. Her first job is to save her family and people from her husband's wrath by honoring her word to both parties regarding her marriage to the sultan. The princess of Tars seems to be a reimagining of the biblical heroine, Esther, who uses her position at the heart of the Babylonian king's court and his affection for her to secure protection for her people and family. The connection between Esther and the princess of Tars is strengthened if we consider part of Esther's prayer before she goes to confront the king about his genocidal decree against the Jews—for the first time, we are given Esther's true thoughts on her marriage to the king: "You know that I hate the glory of the pagans, and abhor the bed of the uncircumcised or of any foreigner. You know that I am under constraint, that I abhor the sign of grandeur which rests on my head when I appear in public; abhor it like a polluted rag, and do not wear it in private" (Esth. 4.C.26-27). Esther does not convert her husband to her faith, but she is instrumental in protecting her people by working within the system as a valued and deferential consort. She is keenly aware of the balance between public performance as the queen of Babylon and the dangers posed by her private identity as a Jew. We see strong echoes of this brand of diplomacy in the princess of Tars's willingness to gain her husband's favor with her acquiescence.

The princess's second job is incidental and spurred on by the birth of the lump of flesh: to convert the masses to Christianity and dissolve the personal religious borders between her and her husband, and between them and their subjects, between her people and her husband's people, once and for all. To accomplish these goals, the princess needs to build trust and at least a semblance of harmony between herself and her husband and his court. The sultan himself is beside himself with joy that she is willing to obey his will and convert to his own religion:

> Þan was þe Soudan glad & bliþe,
> & þanked Mahoun mani siþe
> Þat sche was so biknawe;
> His ioie couþe he noman kiþe. (493-96)

To all appearances, the princess and the sultan have an amicable relationship once the issue of religion is allegedly settled. By consenting to his desires for her to convert, she not only performs the role of a good Christian woman submitting meekly to her husband's desires, but also creates a demilitarized zone between herself and the sultan where they can have relatively open communication.

The romance might be titled *The King of Tars*, but the main character throughout the entire text is clearly the unnamed princess of Tars. She is introduced very early in the romance and described as a typical romance heroine capable of inspiring love and lust from men who have never even seen her but have heard reports of her extraordinary beauty:

> Non feirer woman miȝt ben,
> As white as feþer of swan.
> Þe meiden was schist & bliþe of chere,
> Wiþ rode red so blosme on brere,
> & eyȝen stepe & grey;
> Wiþlowe scholders & white swere.
> Her forto sen was gret preier
> Of princes proud [in] play. (12-19)

The physical description of the princess clearly places her amongst countless other romance heroines of incomparable beauty. The princess's beauty is so remarkable that many princes all over the world who have heard reports of her pray to be able to catch a glimpse of the woman in question. Unfortunately for the princess, one such man is the sultan of Damascus who first asks for her hand in marriage, writing to her father, the King of Tars, that the Sultan is a wealthy suitor who will keep her in luxury: "he wald, houso it bifalle, / His douhter cloþe in riche palle, / & spouse hir wiþ his ring" (28-30) and delivers the ultimatum that if she is not given willingly, "He wald her win in batayl" (32). When the sultan offers for the princess, he does not mention religion at all; as the passage above notes, he merely offers to marry her honorably and assures her father that he is both powerful and rich, worthy of a king's daughter. Further, he establishes that he is unafraid of conflict—he is willing to go to war to have her. Oddly enough, this is not the detail that the king of Tars takes away from the exchange. Instead of focusing on the martial threat or being pleased that he could make such an extraordinarily wealthy and powerful match for his daughter, he frets over his daughter's possible conversion and brings the matter up to her directly, asking, "Waldestow, douhter, for tresour, / Forsake Ihesus our saueour, / þat suffred woundes fiue?" (55-57). He seems concerned that the sultan's great power and wealth might be enough to turn his daughter's head and lead her astray, although she assures him it will not (60-66). Later in the romance, the poet breaks into the narrative to mention mutual concerns regarding intermarriage:

> Wel loþe war a Cristen man
> To wedde an heþen woman
> That leued on fals lawe;
> Als loþ was þat Soudan
> To wed a Cristen woman. (409-413)

Neither Christians nor Saracens are comfortable or open to intermingling. Conversion is going to be a point of conflict, but not in the way medieval audiences would have been trained to expect. In this passage, the poet poses a very interesting inversion of the threat of religious miscegenation. Not only is the Christian princess wary of marrying a pagan, the sultan is equally and rightfully afraid of the contamination she might bring to his court, and so demands that she convert to preserve the religious homogeneity of the Saracen community. There are very light shades of the saint about her even so early in the text—like many a martyred virgin before her, she is appalled at the idea of marrying a pagan, who she calls a "tirant" (64).

The implication drawn from common hagiographical knowledge leaves her and the romance's audience in no doubt that to marry the sultan means conversion, and that he will have the power to force her to convert or send her to her death for her refusal. On a related note, in the Auchinleck, *KT* is clustered with other religious-themed texts, including the hagiographies of *Seynt Mergrete* (Saint Margaret of Antioch) and *Seynt Katerine* (Saint

Catherine of Alexandria). Both accounts of these two virgin martyrs enjoyed great popularity among medieval audiences, as Andrea Hopkins writes, "From the late thirteenth century onwards, the most popular saints' lives were retold independently from the big legendaries, and these were overwhelmingly the lives of virgin martyrs—St Katherine of Alexandria is the most often retold and copied by a considerable margin, with St Margaret of Antioch next" (Hopkins 126). Both women followed a similar path to the princess of Tars, wherein they are menaced and wooed in turns—but unlike the princess, they are ultimately tortured and put to death by Saracen rulers for their refusals to convert. Arguably, the princess of Tars is far more successful in her conversion endeavors because of her ability to adapt and pass as a Saracen until the time is right—in the end, she orchestrates the conversion of a sultan and his entire kingdom for Christianity. In any case, the contrast between the princess and the virgin martyrs raise questions of pragmatism regarding religion vs. secular decisions and a sovereign's duty to his/her people. In terms of romance, even one with hagiographical overtones, this secular pragmatism is to be expected. The princess triumphs because she fulfills the gendered role expected of her, even if she must make the difficult decision to hide her faith. The price of safeguarding her family and people from her volatile suitor is her compliance, although it cannot last. Maintaining even secret difference is not sustainable in the long term.

As mentioned above, the princess's job is to not to die heroically for her faith but to convert others to it. Therefore, we need her alive, we need her pragmatic, and we need stakes high enough to ensure that she does not decide martyrdom is preferable. Jane Gilbert examines the variant texts of the romance and notes the same. She writes,

> each text makes it clear that the Princess would have been morally and generically wrong to have demanded the path of virgin martyrdom at her people's expense, while

the greater Christian community within the text is shown ultimately to profit from her marriage just as in hagiography it does from a virgin martyr's death or from a married saint's refusal of worldliness. Although the poem begins with the opposition, familiar from virgin martyr's lives, between Christ and the pagan suitor, in this case the two turn out to be miraculously compatible, a resolution prefigured in the Princess's erotically charged dream of an aggressive black hound transformed into a white knight who promises her Christ's protection. (116)

Accordingly, the poem makes the loss of life over the princess very clear, as Christian forces are soundly routed and thirty thousand men die in the war (*KT* 211). The idea that the princess is doing the right thing in pretending to convert from Christianity is seemingly radical, because it places the importance of her family and people over religion, the safety of the group over her own sexual purity. The text presents us with the pragmatic idea that martyrdom is only acceptable on an individual or small-group basis; the danger that the kingdom of Tars faces is genocide. The immediate benefit of her surrender is a cease in hostilities. Out of options and facing defeat and abduction, the princess sacrifices herself for her family and people, agreeing to marry the sultan to end the bloodshed:

> Sir, lete me be þe soudans wiif,
> & rere namore cuntek no striif
> As haþ ben here bifore.
> For me haþ mani man ben schent,
> Cites nomen & tounes brent.
> Allas þat ich was bore!
> Fader, y wil serue at wille
> Þe Soudan boþe loude & stille,
> & leue on God almiȝt.
> Bot it so be he schal þe spille,
> & alle þi lond take him tille,
> Wiþ bateyle & wiþ fiȝt.
> Certes y nil no lenger dreye
>
> Þat Cristen folk for me dye.
> It were a diolful siȝt. (223-37)

The princess reveals a practical character trait here—willful deceptiveness, not unlike her Saracen sisters of Floripas and Josian. She is motivated to save her family and people and mentions the sheer amount of damage done to her lands: the razed cities and towns, the danger of being completely overrun and taken over by the sultan, and the thousands of men dead defending her. There is too much to lose here, but she says something very interesting in lines 229-231. She says that she is willing to serve the sultan both "loude & stille, / & leue on God almiʒt." This is an easy passage to misread if we translate the words to modern usage and meanings. According to the online Middle English Dictionary, *loude* means "the backbone, spine," as well as "aloud"; *stille* as a noun means both "peaceful" and "stealthy" while the adj. means "silent"; and *leue* can mean "believe" or "treacherous." In short, there is a lot of double-speak happening in this passage. The princess anticipates the sultan's demand for her conversion, and she knows she will have to agree even if she finds conversion and worshipping other gods repugnant to her faith. However, if she truly intended to obey him both publicly and privately, she could have left it at "loude & stille." But, because she tacks on the reassurance that she will continue to believe in the God almighty (read: the Christian God), she lets the audience know that we should not take her at face value. She tells us not to believe what we are about to see her do, that her conversion will be a political and personal sham. Although this dishonesty—albeit for the good reason of preservation of herself, her family, and her people—might seem incongruous for a Christian heroine, it fits with Czarnowus's idea that the romance sees nothing wrong with the sketchy ethics of conversion:

> Ethical values, such as honesty and truthfulness, undergo relativization: missionary activities of Christians may be carried out stealthily, in the guise of obedient adjustment to the mores of Muslims. The underhand strategy is ennobled by the praiseworthy plans of leading Saracens away from the religion of Mohammad, customarily represented as a crook in medieval tradition. (466)

If the sultan wants her, he can have her, but she will be a snake in the grass and wait for an opportunity to strike. I do not think she has a full plan in this moment—right now she is trying to convince her father to let her go to the sultan to stop the war. In the short term, she is buying time before figuring out what the next move should be. In the meantime, she enters the sultan's court and offers no resistance to anything or anyone she encounters there. Her game has already begun with her outward acquiescence to the sultan's wishes, and she does not let on that she is sorrowful at her situation (394-96). The sultan is overjoyed, and as he promised her father in his initial overture, he has her dressed in the finest clothes: "Into a chaumber sche was ladde, / & richeliche sche was cladde / as heþen wiman were" (382-4). She dons the clothes of her new Saracen court, and begins to look the part of a sultan's consort.

The situation seems dire for the Christian princess, but the text makes it completely clear that the princess's actions throughout the romance, including her deceptions and public worship of Saracen gods, have divine sanction. After she arrives at the sultan's court, the princess dreams of a black hound and is reassured by Christ himself that she has God's help and protection, and that she is being used for a higher purpose (421-56):

> Ihesu, heuen king,
> Spac to hir in manhede,
> In white cloþes, als a kniȝt,
> & seyd to hir, "Mi swete wiȝt,
> No þarf þe noþing drede,
> Of Teruagaunt no of Mahoun.
> Þi lord þat suffred passioun
> Schal help þi at þi need." (449-456).

The dream and the prayers she makes the following morning after her arrival to the court, help her to face her new reality. Of course, after the guarantee of the dream, the sultan makes the demand that surprises no one: convert or he will resume the war against her father (470-80). Clearly, he is expecting resistance on this point, but the princess surprises and delights him with her willing submission to his demand:

> Sir, y nil þe nouȝt greue.
> Teche me now & lat me here

> Hou y schal make mi preire
> When ich on hem beleue.
> To Mahoun ichil me take,
> & Ihesu Crist, mi Lord, forsake. (483-88)

Not only does the princess cheerfully agree to convert to Islam as he requests, she asks him to teach her about her new religion so she will be able to pray correctly. She plays her role superbly, and the sultan is entirely taken in by her deception: "Þe Soudan wende niʒt & day / Þat sche hadde leued opon his lay, / Bot al he was bicouʒt" (511-13). In public, the princess converts to her new religion entirely and without reservation. No one can sway her or change her mind from her decision (509-10). Yet, she remains Christian in the privacy of her quarters and prays quietly: "For when sche was bi hirselue on / To Ihesu sche made hir mon, / Þat alle þis world haþ wrouʒt" (514-16). In her book, *Representing Difference in the Medieval and Modern Orientalist Romance*, Amy Burge writes, "This performance of Saracen religious custom marks the princess visually and performatively as a Saracen, creating a disjunction between her external Saracen appearance and her internal Christianity" (124). The princess can set aside her own distaste enough to perform her role as the new Saracen queen of the court, but this "incoherence" (125) as Burge calls it, ultimately results in a lump-child and ends the princess's ability to pass as something she is not.

The second major point of interest in the King of Tars is the formless lump-child that the princess delivers. In her essay "Marking Religion on the Body: Saracens, Categorization, and *The King of Tars*," Calkin writes about the blurring of religious and even biological boundaries and identities, from the mis-categorization of the princess as a Saracen because she publicly (though not privately) converts to Islam (224), to the birth of the lump of flesh. Of the lump-child, she writes,

> The child of the unconverted Christian princess and her Saracen husband constitutes a being that unites Christian and Saracen identities and therefore defies religious

> identification. Theoretically, the child offers the possibility of no longer needing to concern oneself with religious categories and sociocultural differences since it conflates such categories and differences. As the text examines challenges of differentiating individuals based on their physical appearance and behavior, it thus explores the possibility of an existence that eludes religious categorization and differentiation altogether. (226)

However, since the child is disturbing to look at and does not appear even remotely human, the text reaffirms the need for categorization and boundaries. Until the lump of flesh is born, the borders between religions and cultures had been allowed to collapse and intermingle: "the failed religious identification of individuals produces a biological indeterminacy that horrifies and troubles the communities to which the child belongs" (227). Perhaps the child, as unnerving as it is to look upon, is also comforting to the medieval Christian audience of the romance; it serves as proof of the importance of difference and provides further evidence that the princess has not truly converted to Islam after all, because the confusions of identity resulted in a confusion of flesh. Jane Gilbert interprets the child not only as a physical sign of the outcome of miscegenation between two people of different faiths, but also as the text's reaffirmation of the sultan's subhuman, even bestial status. She writes,

> the child's animal side suggests a sub-human aspect to its father. This is accentuated in *KT*, where both narrator and characters repeatedly compare the Sultan and his men to animals ... Before their christening, father and son are deemed sub-human to the degree that each represents only the crude form of a human being, lacking that spiritual dimension which properly distinguishes humans from the other animals. Baptism refines the animal-heathen substance to create a superior being—hairless, white, fully human (104-105).

The romance questions what it means to be human and argues that to be human is to be Christian. The sultan and the lump-child cannot be human unless they are Christianized, and the princess makes this entirely clear after the lump is transformed into a child. The transformation is nothing short of miraculous. The lump of flesh she delivers is not even vaguely recognizable as human:

> & when þe child was ybore,
> Wel sori wimin were þerefore,
> For lim no hadde it non.
> Bot as a rond of flesche yschore
> In chaumber it lay hem bifore
> Wiþouten blod & bon.
> For sorwe þe leuedi wald dye
> For it hadde noiþer nose no eye,
> Bot lay ded as þe ston. (576-85)

The princess and her women are aggrieved because the child is not human, and neither is it alive. The lump-child has no limbs, blood, bones, or facial features. The lump-child is monstrous. The sultan accuses the princess of being at fault for not truly believing in his gods (590-594). The princess does not either confirm or deny his accusation, but retorts,

> ȝif Mahoun & Iouin can
> Make it fourmed after a man
> Wiþ liif & limes ariȝt,
> Bi Ihesu Crist, þat þis warld wan,
> Y schal leue þe better þan
> Þat þai ar ful of miȝt. (613-18)

Without directly admitting that her conversion was false, she sets a challenge before the sultan: if his gods can turn the lump-child into a living, breathing, normal child, then she will be swayed by the miracle into complete faith that his gods are truly legitimate and more powerful. The sultan takes the challenge and presents the lump-child to his idols to no avail. Enraged the sultan destroys the idols and says, "Mine godes no may help me nouȝt. / Þe deuel hem sett afere!" (671-2). The princess calmly suggests that since he tried his gods, that he allow her to try hers (675-84). The sultan echoes her earlier pronouncement that if a miracle should happen that he will convert to her religion (685-96).

The princess immediately begins the preparations by searching the dungeons for a Christian priest, and makes sure to check the credentials of the priest when he is brought before her: "Artow a prest? / Tel me soþe ȝif þat tow best. / Canstow of Cristen lore?" (727-

9). Satisfied with his affirmative answer the princess tells him that together they will "make Cristen men of houndes" (743). The priest begins preparations for the lump's baptism:

> A feir vessel he tok þat tide,
> & hali water he gan make.
> At missomer tide þat ded was don
> þurth help of God, þat sitt in trone,
> As y ʒou tel may.
> Þe prest toke þe flesche anon,
> & cleped it þe name of Ion
> In worþschip of þe day
> & when þat is cristened was,
> It hadde liif & lim & fas. (767-76)

The baptism is not as simple as a priest splashing water on a child. The holy water must be made, the child must be named, and then the baptism occurs. Once the ritual is complete, the monstrous lump-child transforms into a living, breathing child who possess all the normal limbs and features.

Although the lump-child is equally distressing to all parties, it also presents an exploitable opportunity for the princess to use as leverage. When the child is baptized and becomes human, "Feirer child miʒt non be bore" (781), the princess now has a priceless bargaining chip she never had before, because she produced the one thing any king wants above all: a healthy son and heir. Immediately she asserts the authority granted to her through the miracle by denying the sultan paternity of the child and fellowship with his new family: "Bot þou were cristned so it is / Þou no hast no part þeron, ywis, / Noiþer of þe child ne of me" (815-16). As Burge points out, the princess uses Christianity to redefine the boundaries around herself and her child, excluding the sultan from the relationship on grounds of religious difference (Burge 129). Moreover, she no longer fears reprisal for her disobedience to him. He has seen with his own eyes the miracle baptism has wrought on a lifeless lump of flesh. Unlike the typical antagonist of a virgin martyr's hagiography, the sultan has the good sense to know when he has been outplayed and takes the miracle as evidence that he should adjust his worldview because his wife is in the right. Hopkins observes that this vindication is common in romance:

> a consideration of the romance featuring pious heroines in the light of their saintly prototypes shows that they are not entirely meek and passive. Like the virgin martyrs, they choose to do right and accept the suffering consequent on their choice. They speak out boldly and call a sin a sin. They are in firm occupation of the moral high ground; no matter how often they have been falsely accused during the course of their adventures, they are always vindicated at the end of the romance and their father, husbands, or other adversaries are shown to be in the wrong. (137)

However, the heroine's vindication does not come at the end of the romance. The miracle of the lump-child has shown the sultan the error of his ways, and the princess's ultimatum that he shall not be with her or the child until he converts is added pressure in case he tries to renege on their agreement. She reclaims the authority she originally gave up to him for the sake of peace, and it is his turn to make concessions to her.

The sultan acts according to his word and agrees to baptism, which the text makes even more complicated and includes interventions and ritual preparations on the sultan's behalf from both the priest and the princess. The lump-child's baptism was straightforward because the infant cannot be expected to know his religion—the same cannot be said for the sultan's baptism. The text's rite is more complex when it involves the conscious decision to convert as an adult. In a reversal of her own fake conversion, the princess first instructs the sultan in the Christian articles of faith at his own request (829-76). Then the priest must give his blessing, which he does: "Sir ich am redi here / Wiþ alle þe pouwer þat y can / Forto make þe Cristen man" (893). Next the text outlines the process of making holy water (901-12). Once the ritual begins, something happens that erases any lingering doubts the sultan might have regarding his choice to convert: a miracle is wrought on himself—his skin turns from black to white:

> The Cristen prest hiʒt Cleophas;
> He cleped þe Soudan of Damas
> After his owhen name.
> His hide, þat blac & loþely was,
> Al white bicom, þurth Godes gras,
> & clere wiþouten blame.
> & when þe Soudan seye þat siʒt
> Þan leued he wele on God almiʒt;
> His care went to game.
> & when þe prest hadde alle yseyd,
> & haly water on him leyd,
> To chaumber þai went ysame. (925-36)

It is interesting to note that the actual baptism comes after the sultan's whitewashing, which occurs as soon as he is granted a Christian name. Until now, the text has not given the sultan a name, merely a title. I read this moment as part of the *process* of conversion and of baptism. The sultan is not converted or baptized all at once. In fact, the romance makes it clear that a baptism (particularly an adult baptism of a willing participant) is not spontaneous; it is a ritual that requires authority, knowledge, and careful preparation.

The romance heightens the dramatic tension by giving the sultan ample time to change his mind or back out of his agreement with the princess, but when morning dawns, the sultan goes to the priest and disrobes to receive his baptism (923-4). I argue that the disrobing of the sultan is key here; he is shedding his old identity in layers to gain a new one. First, he sheds his Eastern clothes. Second, he sheds his name (which the text does not tell us) to gain another, Cleophas (925). Third, his skin transforms from black to white. Only then, after all these things have happened, does the sultan completely and unreservedly convert. He is no longer going through with baptism because he is honor-bound. He is not undergoing a false conversion to make the princess happy, the way she pretended to convert for him. He genuinely believes in the Christian god, which allows the priest to complete the ritual. As soon as he is finished, he goes to his wife in her chamber and she is beside herself with joy at his conversion. Whereas before she tolerated his existence, she is now delighted with her husband now that they are of the same religion: "For þat hir lord was cristned so / away was went al hir wo; / Hir ioie gan wax al newe" (946-8). Furthermore, now the princess lays verbal claim to her husband. Before, she referred to him respectfully to his face as "sir" (483, 603, 675, 682, 813, 843,) but once she began to lay groundwork for his conversion, he becomes her lord (698, 946, 949). If she redrew the boundaries of their difference to exclude him before, she redraws them again to include him as he comes closer to her faith. Furthermore, she draws him into her own family and the romance ends in a reversal of the way it begins. At the princess's behest, the converted sultan reaches out to his new father-in-law, the king of Tars, to help him convert his country to Christianity by the sword (950-54). If the beginning of the romance saw the Christian armies soundly defeated, the romance ends with the Christian armies victorious, beheading the Saracens who refuse to convert (1235). Ultimately, the princess facilitates the conversion not only of her husband, but also of her new country.

Conclusion

Women, both Saracen and Christian, in medieval crusading romances are integral to conversion and legitimizing the crusade endeavors. The Saracen princess's conversion and amorous attachment to a Christian knight gives the Western heroes a stamp of approval in their crusade. They do not just go East to win land, honor, and wealth, but they gain all of that and manage to seduce the beautiful and powerful Eastern women to their cause as well. If the Western knightly heroes distinguish themselves as militarily superior on the battlefield, their seduction of such women (or indeed, their seduction of him) prove the knights as superior off the battlefield as well. The Saracen princesses who convert embark on a journey to find a new place in their adopted Christian communities, a prospect that is easier than it sounds. Floripas disappears from the romance before we can see any changes in her personality, but Josian shows the struggle to become the demure Christian woman that Bevis wants.

The Christian damsels who marry Saracens prove to be powerful in their own right—the Saracen princess converts only herself to legitimize her Christian lover's exploits, but the Christian princess of Tars has broader expectations. Although the complete conversion of the sultan and his kingdom is the endgame of *KT*, the romance is presented as a pragmatic answer to the Saracen problem, one that balances martial deeds with the princess's deft political hand. The princess is a lovely double agent, sent directly to the heart of the Saracen court to change it from within. Her ability to adapt to the Saracen court, at least publicly, places her in position to win her husband's confidence and later to convert him and, by extension, his entire country to Christianity. The Christian damsel is an exercise in soft conversion tactics because all she must do is convert her husband to begin the process of facilitating conversions. Once the sultan is converted, he takes up the mantle of hard conversion tactics and converts his entire nation by force.

Conversion is used in these romances as a possible method of gaining and maintaining a foothold in the Middle East, because it focuses on incorporating the Other into the Christian fold. Like *Sir Isumbras*, the goal of the *KT* is not just establishing a new Christian nation in place of the old Saracen regime, but also creating a dynasty to continue Christianity. We see shades of dynastic intentions in *Bevis* as well, as Josian's son Guy inherits Josian's ancestral home of Armenia and forcibly converts it with his father (4006-4020). The romances in this chapter argue for the necessity of women in the conversion process, because all of them have a role in legitimizing Western crusades to the Middle East, whether they do so by choosing a Christian knight above all other suitors (and thus symbolically proving to medieval audiences the supremacy of the West) or helping create and perpetuate a Christian dynasty.

Chapter 3: Sir Palomides, Malory's Sisyphean Saracen Knight

The Arthurian tradition is frequently concerned with early ideas of empire, so it makes sense that it would occasionally turn its attention to the Middle East and to crusading endeavors. The fact that Saracens have a presence in the Arthurian canon—even early Latinate Arthurian canon—is not surprising. However, what is surprising is that the fifteenth-century Thomas Malory would cut through centuries of unflattering representation of Saracens and of the Middle East to craft one of the most complex literary Saracens in medieval English literature, if not one of the most realistic characters in the entirety of his *Morte Darthur*. Sir Palomides, whose main story arc occurs in the "The Book of Tristram," is a fascinating portrayal of a Saracen knight on the fringes of the Arthurian court and community. Palomides demonstrates the difficulties of succeeding in Arthurian knighthood by falling short of the seemingly impossible standards set by Lancelot and Tristram. He is unique not in the way he succeeds but in the ways he fails in love, in prowess, and in courtly behavior. He even struggles with religion and what it means to be a Christian; his entire journey is about becoming a good Christian knight.

According to Valerie B. Johnson, Palomides is first introduced in the thirteenth century Old French Prose *Tristan*, a text which serves as one of Malory's sources for the *Morte* (par. 1). The character does not appear in any other romances except the translations of the Prose *Tristan*, and only enters the English tradition in the *Morte* (par. 5).[26] Malory's Sir Palomides is the unrelenting pursuer of the Questing Beast, the unrequited lover of Isode,

---

[26] Johnson provides a brief but comprehensive history of the character of Palomides. She indicates that after Malory, Palomides did not appear in another text until William Fulford's "The Lament of Palomides" (1862), and then in a few texts of the early 20th century. The character, connected as he is to the Tristan tradition, was completely ignored in Lord Alfred Tennyson's *The Idylls of the King* (1885) and while T.H. White does include Palomides in his *The Once and Future King* (1958), White does not include Tristan except in passing, and "with his purpose as a foil to Tristan dissolved, [Palomides] becomes a buffoon" (par. 6).

one of the best knights in the world, and a Saracen on the precarious edge of conversion.

Nina Dulin-Mallory writes,

> The fact that even after the rest of his family had been baptized we have the unredeemed Palomides to observe is significant in the *Morte*: this Saracen will fight in battles every one of which puts him in peril of a mortal wound that would send his soul to hell; we have also to observe him as a Saracen lover whose great passion for Isolt is hopeless because she loves a greater and Christian knight; and we observe him as a Saracen who takes up the most puzzling quest of the entire *Morte Darthur*—the search for the Questing Beast. (169)

In other words, Malory gives us a complex, multi-dimensional portrayal of a Saracen knight who is caught in the tangles of religion, love, and knighthood. Part of the drama of this character is the expectation that at least some of his issues will be resolved—audiences see his rise in fame and prowess, see him risk his life and very soul in battle, and see his endless pining for Isode. Sir Palomides complicates the text's treatment of honor and knighthood because he very nearly holds his own against the major heroes of Arthurian canon and presents one of the most complex images of a Saracen in Middle English romance. He is Other, the text reminds us often, but that Otherness is not nearly as clear cut as in the crusading romances. For example, the text mostly respects him. While other romances refer to Saracens as heathen hounds and by other rude epithets, Palomides is presented to us as a man who, while flawed, is not inherently evil, stupid, or cowardly. His struggles and frustrations are relatable. On the one hand, he is representative of the ideal Saracen knight that Christians would love to officially add to their number, *a la* Ferumbras: "Malory's Sir Palomydes functions as the typical worthy pagan antagonist known in the European heroic traditions from the twelfth century forward" (Wheeler 69). He is a good knight, and almost indistinguishable from his Christian peers; he lacks the monstrosity of the undesirable

Saracens (such as the giants) who will not be absorbed into the Christian community.[27] On the other hand, Palomides is a destabilizing force in the text.[28] As Maria Sachiko Cecire writes, "Palomydes's example throws doubt upon the inherent superiority of Christianity by demonstrating that it does not always assure superior knighthood" (139). He is commonly acknowledged as the fourth best knight after Lancelot, Tristram, and Lamorak (Malory 435). Although unconverted, Palomides is already as much a part of the Arthurian community as he is ever going to be, as evidenced by his baptism and exit from the text occurring at the very *end* of his story (Malory 507-511). We never get to see if any miraculous transformations are wrought on his body or personality as we do with the sultan in *The King of Tars*. Palomides merely resumes his fruitless hunt of the Questing Beast and returns in cameo mentions in tournaments and as one of Lancelot's faithful knights at the end of the romance when loyalties between knights are fraying and the kingdom is falling apart (Malory 700).

This chapter will focus primarily on Sir Palomides. First, I will discuss Palomides's spiritual liminality, and the way another Saracen knight, Corsabryne, acts as both a mirror for Palomides as well as a warning for the dangers of dying unconverted to Christianity. Although Palomides professes to believe as a Christian and exhibits no Muslim beliefs in the text, he does not automatically convert as one would be trained to expect from crusading romances. Instead, Palomides delays his official conversion and takes a vow to fight seven battles for Christ before his baptism. Second, I will examine Palomides and love and gender,

---

[27] See Chapter 2, "The Saracen Princess." Also see, de Weever's *Sheba's Daughters*, and Jeffrey Jerome Cohen's *Of Giants: Sex, Monsters and the Middle Ages*.

[28] See Christine Pyle's essay, "Sacramental Unity for a Saracen: Malory's Conflicted Knight Palomides" for a good, in-depth discussion of the discord and journey to wholeness in Palomides's character and in "The Book of Tristram."

particularly in terms of his emotional outbursts of grief and his failure to gain the love of his sovereign lady, Isode. Finally, I will look at Palomides's fight to fit into the Arthurian chivalric community: to gain worship and acceptance into the Round Table, to win the fellowship of his knightly rivals, and to live up to the seemingly impossible ideals of knighthood.

Saracens in Arthurian Texts

Before I can begin a detailed discussion of Palomides, it is prudent to examine more generally some of the Saracens and Middle Eastern influences that exist across Arthurian literature in order to get a sense of what makes Palomides unique in the overall Arthurian tradition. While Arthurian literature is mostly concerned with Britain and to a lesser extent continental Europe, it is not uncommon for Saracens and other elements of the East to appear in various texts. There are Eastern/crusading influences in one of the two full-length surviving Latin prose romances on the Matter of Britain: the relatively obscure romance known as *De ortu Waluuanii nepotis Arturi*, or, *The Rise of Gawain, Nephew of Arthur* (*RG*).[29] The romance exists in only one manuscript, the London British Museum Cotton Faustina B VI, 23r-38r. Curiously, the romance keeps company not with other romances or entertainments but instead with an assortment of miscellaneous historical documents: papal letters, financial records, obituaries, annals, etc. (Day 24). According to Mildred Leake Day, scholars have been debating the possible date of the romance since the nineteenth century. Some believe it is a late twelfth century text, others think it is comfortably thirteenth century, and arguments have been made that it might be as late as the fourteenth century. However,

---

[29] The edition of the text I am referencing is Mildred Leake Day's edition, which features a facing Latin-English translation. This is the version of the romance that was also included in the third edition of the anthology *The Romance of Arthur*, edited by Lacy and Wilhelm.

Day argues that "a closer examination of the text confirms a twelfth-century point of view. This includes the earlier Arthurian characters, surcoat and helmet, settings in Jerusalem and Caerleon, ship structure and modification, and passage through the Straits of Gibraltar without making landfall until the coast of France"[30] (10). The main action in the *RG* centers on the episode wherein Gawain travels from Rome to Christian Jerusalem to battle the King of Persia's giant champion to decide who controls Jerusalem. The romance is very loosely based on an actual fifth-century war between the Persians and the Eastern Roman Empire, although it does take temporal liberties (15). Indeed, a feature of romance is the inclination towards atemporality. This allows romance, as a genre, a certain amount of flexibility or even a fusion of "once upon a time" and recent events. While that Persian-Roman war happened long before Islam, Gawain's heroic battle for the fate of Jerusalem must have had some contemporary resonance for twelfth- or thirteenth-century audiences for whom a string of failed crusades was recent history.

The *RG* romance is not necessarily a traditional crusade text. In fact, it is not typical at all, even if we cast aside the ahistorical difficulties of the events described above. The attitude toward war is even markedly different than many of the texts I have discussed so far. Instead of slaughtering each other in a frenzy of *deus vult* enthusiasm, the writer highlights the extent that both parties work to sue for peace before the fighting even begins:

> [W]ar broke out between the King of Persia and the Christians remaining in Jerusalem. When the day chosen by the Persians for battle had dawned, the besieging

---

[30] The Straits of Gibraltar proved both valuable and a dangerous entrance to the Mediterranean, and for much of the 12th century, many ports in Muslim-held Spain and Africa were closed to Christian shipping (Leake 10). Furthermore, as Archibald R. Lewis points out, between the unfavorable winds and current, and the possibility of interception by hostile military fleets on the Atlantic side of the Straits, many northern European ships who entered the Straits did not sail back out. Lewis points out that ships from northern Europe were Scandinavian (they utilized oars and were renowned for their maritime skill), or did not have commercial aims (instead focused on piracy, pilgrimage, etc.), and most ships were abandoned in the Mediterranean because their crews returned home overland (140, 144). At least by the later Middle Ages, as the *Reconquista* of Spain continued, the ports were opened and duties more affordable.

> formations of both cavalry and foot drawn up into an enormous force produced a spectacle of terror; and by separate ranks, step by step, they drew near to battle. Already the trumpets were being sounded, the bowstrings tautened, the lances couched, and the chief centurions were impatient to join in hand-to-hand combat, yet at this moment, those more mature in both age and wisdom of both sides were meeting in council. When these men considered the clash of such huge numbers and such great force could not take place without an enormous loss of life, they proceeded between the lines, restrained the first attack, and then sent officials to discuss the conditions of peace with either side. (*RG* 67)

There are a couple points of interest packed into this one excerpt. First, no explanation is given for the war, but we can surmise that it is at least in part motivated by religion. The writer mentions "the Christians remaining in Jerusalem" which, if we are considering the text in the light of the early crusades, seems to suggest that perhaps most of the crusading forces have already gone home after securing the Holy City, or that the Christians have become a strong enough political force that they can wage war. Regardless, the writer is very specific in saying that it is the Persians going to war against the Christians. It raises the question of how cosmopolitan Jerusalem is: why only the Christians? Secondly, the writer draws the tension of the scene to its breaking point. The pre-battle imagery is intense and visceral: the sounding of the trumpets, the armies lined up ready and eager to go to war, the creak of the bowstrings pulled back, the bracing of lances in preparation of a charge or defense—all it would take is someone sneezing at this moment to start the carnage. However, instead of encouraging war, the ruling powers that be are trying to stop it. Considering that the major crusade texts thus far examined in this dissertation (*Firumbras, Sir Isumbras, The King of Tars, Richard Coer de Lion,* etc.) all feature scenes of extensive warfare and huge losses on all sides without so much as a murmur in protest beforehand at the loss of life, the fact that this text pointedly illustrates the diplomatic lengths to which both sides are *working together* up to the very last minute to broker peace before the battle is nothing short of extraordinary.

At the same time, the text's insistence that Jerusalem is in Christian hands echoes a common medieval belief regarding the true ownership of the Holy City. As Norman Daniel writes, "Every reference to lands that had once been Christian, and particularly to the Holy Land, must be understood to have been made on the assumption that these were lost provinces belonging by right to the Latin Church" (109). Interestingly, the text does not mention a pope, who would be the de facto leader of the Roman (or Latin) Church, but places ownership of the lands and the responsibility of its defense and fate on the Roman emperor instead (*RG* 67). The truce agreement brought to Rome for the emperor's assent is an invitation to a trial by single combat. Both parties agree that whichever champion wins will decide who has control of Jerusalem. The Roman emperor, as the acknowledged ruler of Jerusalem, agrees to Gawain's request to send him to be his champion in the duel. Religious overtones begin to bleed through with Gawain's speech: "war is declared by the infidels not only against you and the Roman people, but against the Christian faith. I entreat Your Highness that you grant now what you bestowed on me, so that I may not only receive your promised boon but also avenge the honor of the Roman people and the reverence for religion" (67). Gawain sees the duel as being a deciding factor not just for the physical control of the city of Jerusalem, but a defense of the honor of the Roman people and the Christian faith. The Persians are not explicitly named as Saracens or Muslims (again, the romance is ostensibly set in a time before the advent of the Islamic faith), but to a late twelfth or early thirteenth century audience for whom crusading was either very recent history or an ongoing part of life, the battle over Jerusalem between Christian and pagan armies would have inescapable overtones of Muslim-Christian conflict.

Gawain faces the giant, Gormundus, and defeats him after three days of combat, which lends Gawain Christ-like overtones—he does not descend into hell to save souls, but he does battle a giant monster for the city and the souls of the Christian soldiers for three days, emerging victorious at the end. The Persian army, constrained by the agreement, are forced to admit failure and go home: "Once their defender had been given over to death, the pagans yielded to the sovereignty of the pact with the Romans according to the agreed conditions: peace confirmed, hostages given, heavy reparations imposed. The enemy troops retired in confusion to their own country" (107). The episode, carefully negotiated in terms of shared diplomacy, as well as honor and violence, ends without further loss or bloodshed and peace returns to the region. I would go so far as to say this text is subversive and offers a quiet critique of the crusades, by suggesting that open warfare is not necessarily the best or only way to settle differences. The subversion is even more extraordinary if we agree with Day that this is a twelfth century work (or even early thirteenth century), when the success of the First Crusade and the failures of subsequent crusades would be firm in the Western consciousness.

As mentioned above, *RG* is a Latin romance set temporally before Islam, but still has overtones of East-West conflict that would be familiar to the romance's audience. Although the *Alliterative Morte* and the *Morte Darthur* engage the most with Saracens, there are some other slightly-lesser known Middle English Arthurian romances that also include Saracens or references to crusading, including *Sir Degrevant* and *Perceval of Galles*. The romance, *Sir Degrevant* (*SD*), is tangentially Arthurian. Written sometime during the late fourteenth to early-fifteenth century, the romance exists in two manuscripts, the Findern and Thornton MSS (*Middle English Romance Database*). The beginning of the romance is very clear about

Sir Degrevant's place in the Arthurian world, even if the rest of the romance is about a local drama:

> With Kyng Arrtor, y wene
> And wyth Gwennor the queen,
> [Degrevant] was known for kene,
> That comelych knyght,
> In Hethenesse and in Spayne,
> In ffraunce and in Bryttayne,
> With Persevalle and Gawayne
> ...
> Forthy they name hem that stounde
> A knyght of tabulle Round,
> As maked is in the mappe-mounde
> In storye ffull ryght. (17-23, 29-32)

Sir Degrevant is not one of the most well-known knights of the Round Table, but the poem is careful to establish him as a worthy knight. He has a reputation for ferocity ("was known for kene"). He has been fighting in wars abroad—his time in "Hethenesse" and Spain both point towards his participation in crusading endeavors. Although the crusades themselves would be mostly over at the time of the romance's writing, the *Reconquista*[31] of Spain was not complete until the very end of the fifteenth century. Finally, although Degrevant himself might be a more obscure knight of the Round Table, he keeps company with two of its most famous knights: Perceval and Gawain. The prestige of their fellowship enhances Degrevant's own honor and reputation.

During one campaign abroad, Degrevant is summoned home by his steward because of domestic problems with one of Degrevant's neighbors, an earl who is plundering Degrevant's land and killing his foresters (100-114). The messenger finds Degrevant in the

---

[31] The Muslims conquered and held much of Spain and Portugal (stopping just shy of Castile) from 718 and through the next three centuries. In the mid-eleventh century, the Christian Spanish rulers in the northwest of Spain and those living under Muslim rule rebelled, leading to a gradual loss of territory as Christians reclaimed territory. The fall of the last Muslim holdout of Granada happened in 1492. This period of centuries-long conflict is called the *Reconquista* (Najjaj).

vanguard of the war in Granada—the southeast of Spain and the last Muslim holding to fall in 1492—and the knight immediately rushes home (130-32). The ongoing war serves as backdrop in the romance, as do the Eastern influences. When Degrevant sees the earl's daughter leaving Mass, she is wearing a jeweled dress that includes costly imported pearls lining the front of her bodice: "With a front endent / With peyrl of Orient, / Out of Syprus was sent" (649-51). The romance does not mention whether the earl himself has been to the Mediterranean or the Middle East, but the Cyprus connection functions as a stereotyped shorthand of the earl's extreme wealth. As discussed in the first chapter in this dissertation, ideas of the East often included fantasies of remarkable wealth, particularly in the Byzantium. This detail about the Earl's wealth makes him seem even more of a villain: he is not plundering Degrevant's lands for any reason other than greed. The Earl is content to destroy someone else's property and the income from that property to enhance his own.

The romance is circular. We first meet Degrevant while he is on the front lines in southern Spain. Once he returns home to handle his irascible neighbor and sets his eyes on his neighbor's lovely daughter, crusading no longer has a hold on him. While Degrevant is wooing or happily married to Melidor, he is content to stay at home. When she dies after thirty years of marriage, Degrevant returns to the fighting in the Holy Land:

> And sene sche dyed, y undurstond,
> He seysed hys eyr with hys hond,
> And went into the Holy Lond,
> Heven be hys mede!
> At Port Gaffe was he slon,
> Forjustyd with a soudon (1893-98)

The end of the romance returns Degrevant back where it found him in the beginning: off on crusade. He does not intend to come back this time because he hands over all his possessions and holdings to his heir and returns to the Holy Land where he is ultimately slain in combat with a sultan. Dying in a crusade is a common end for many honorable knights who have finished their domestic duties. Once their major reason for living and service is gone (whether it be loyalty to Arthur or to their wife) the old guard of knights often leave on fatal missions to the Holy Land, after all, this is the fate of four of the surviving knights in Malory's *Morte*:

> For the Frensshe book maketh mencyon—and is auctorysed—that syr Bors, syr Ector, syr Blamour and syr Bleoberis went into the Holy Lande, thereas Jesu Cryst was quycke and deed. And anon as they had stablysshed theyr londes, for, the book saith, so syr Launcelot commanded them for to do or ever he passyd oute of thys world, there these foure knyghtes dyd many batayles upon the myscreantes, or Turks. And there they dyed upon a Good Fryday for Goddess sake. (726)

The last survivors of the Round Table are left at loose ends because everything and everyone they knew before is dead. For Malory, who argues against "somme Englysshe bookes" (725) idea that the knights would remain in a place they no longer truly belong, swears that the French book is the authority on the matter. Sir Degrevant is no different. With his duties discharged, he is free to return to the battlefield. I read this as a way for writers to maintain the honor and integrity of their heroes, by giving them the best kind of death in the service of God at the end of their romance, thus allowing them to serve king, lady, and God, or any combination thereof.

Perceval of Galles (*PG*) exists in one manuscript, the Thornton MS. The romance is dated somewhere between 1300-1340 (Norako, "Perceval of Galles"). It is not the typical Percival romance that one would expect. As Norako writes,

> Often typed as 'crude' or 'unsophisticated' romance, Perceval of Galles is the earliest English version of the Perceval narrative. The most striking difference between it an [sic] continental versions lies in the complete absence of the famous grail quest. Instead, the emphasis in the romance lies on Perceval's development from a 'fool of the field' to a chivalrous knight, and his many exploits and adventures along the way. ("Perceval of Galles").

The romance is very neatly contained. Percival does not pursue the Grail in this tale; in fact, the Grail is never mentioned. Furthermore, the romance ends on a happy note, with Percival as a successful and wealthy king, married to the woman he saved from the sultan, and reunited with his mother. The romance spares Percival the usual consequences of his foolish behavior and selfishness; no one important to Percival dies, and all his wrongs are righted to satisfaction in the end.

Critics seem to be ambivalent about the romance and have varied things to say about the purposes of the tight structure of *PG*. In discussing the story form of *PG*, Ad Putter argues that while the romance might be considered "crude" in terms of style when it is compared with its predecessors like Chretien de Troyes's unfinished French *Conte de Graal*, and Wolfram von Eschenbach's German *Parzival*, the neatness of the English version of the story is possibly the result of being performed by professional entertainers who need to be able to memorize the poem for recitation (173). Yin Liu, however, argues, "If, as seems likely, the English poet worked from firsthand knowledge of Chretien's poem, these radical changes to the story must be regarded as deliberate and purposeful. Indeed, the neatness and care evident in the narrative structure of Sir Perceval point to a poet who pays attention to detail" (81). Caroline D. Eckhardt considers the romance as ultimately a comedy, "the poet's attitude toward his romance material is one of happy gusto, with many a belly-laugh, several times a snort of amusement, but not complicated, sophisticated, quiet jokes, no literary parody" (207). Whatever one thinks of the romance, be it a succinct rewrite of the *Conte* for memorization and performance, a tidy little romance written with careful detail, or a chivalric comedy, for my purposes the romance is interesting because of its inclusion of multiple

Saracens: the Saracen army, the sultan Gollerotherame, and the sultan's giant brother who attempts to woo Percival's mother.

Percival is still new to his chivalric career when he learns about the desperate plight of the lady Lufamour of Maydenland. Her messenger arrives at Percival's uncle's castle on his way to Arthur's court to ask for help to defeat the Saracens (973-1004). The situation is dire enough that the lady has vowed to kill herself rather than be forcibly wed to the sultan (997-1000). Percival decides to help her and rides forth to find and kill the sultan who is taking the lady's lands and threatening to also take her unwilling body in marriage. Percival seeks single combat with the sultan, even going so far as riding into the sultan's army and saying to the soldiers,

> I am hedir come
> For to see a Sowdane;
> In faythe, right sone he sall be slane,
> And I myght hym ken.
> If I hym oghte ken may,
> To-morne, when it es lighted aye
> Than sall we togedir playe
> With wapyns unryde. (1153-60)

In other words, Percival demands that the Saracens take him to their leader so he can challenge him to combat and kill him. Although, he does not quite seem to grasp everything that is happening or who his enemy is. Instead of asking to see *the* sultan, he asks for *a* sultan, as though any sultan will do, instead of the one currently distressing the lady. Percival's generalizing of the sultan, while humorous, underscores the stereotyping at work in the romance. The sultan is but one generic representation of the fear of the Other, the foreign influence that wants to take land and women. The romance is an interesting juxtaposition to most crusade romances; clearly Christian knights going to war in the Middle

East and seducing Middle Easter women is perfectly acceptable, but *PG* shows the English's profound discomfort that comes from being on the receiving end of such colonial endeavors.

Unlike the crusade romances where the invading force is victorious, *PG* does not grant the marauding sultan or his forces victory over the West. Percival's "take me to your leader" pronouncement goes about as well as anyone would expect, and the Saracens immediately set upon Percival. The entire scene and the ensuing battle reads like macabre slapstick humor, wherein Percival decimates the sultan's army on the field outside the castle:

> Now he strykes for the nonys,
> Made the Sarazenes hede-bones
> Hoppe als dose hayle-stones
> Abowtte one the gres (1189-92)

The description of the carnage—specifically, the severed heads surrounding Percival like hail-stones—seems to be more funny than grisly. Percival himself, with his raw strength and untrained fighting style, is not really a man or knight, even if he wears the trappings of one. The text even continues to refer to him as "childe" (1165). Rather, he becomes an unstoppable force of nature. His goal is to fight and kill the sultan, and if he must eliminate an entire army to get to the sultan, he will. Later, when he is inside the castle being questioned by the curious lady Lufamour, he is remarkably blasé about the number of bodies left in his wake. He did not come to kill all of them, just the sultan. But he goes on to say, "thay ne wolde noght late me go; / Thaire lyfes there refte I" (1299-1300). The army became collateral damage in Percival's quest because they engaged him. Percival is clearly unaware of the way warfare works; he seems to think that if only one man is the problem, then he needs only engage with that one man. The romance describes Perceval as thoughtlessly impulsive "Siche wilde gerys hade he mo" (1353). After he kills the small army left outside Lady Lufamour's castle, Percival is so tired that he does not even care for his own life but picks a quiet spot on the battlefield to sleep only to be discovered in the morning by a sentinel (1198-1220). He does not see the Saracen army as human but merely objects that have gotten in the way of his goal, and he certainly does not see anything wrong with taking a nap amidst all the dead on the battlefield when there is a perfectly good castle behind him that would be glad to offer him hospitality. As a knight, the recalcitrant and straightforward Percival has quite a bit to learn.

When the sultan finally returns from his hunting trip (1133) and finds his men dead, Percival finally gets his chance to fight and defeat the sultan. Once the sultan is dead, Percival finds himself in possession of everything the sultan wanted: the lady Lufamour, her riches, and her lands. The newly minted knight becomes a king (1734-40). Percival is not a subtle man, and the romance is not particularly subtle either: the lady is the ruler of a place called Maidenland. The invading Saracen sultan is not just trying to conquer a single lady, but is threatening an institution of Christian, European maidenhood. The sultan's defeat and Percival's subsequent marriage to the lady removes the threat of foreign, non-Christian influence. Percival himself becomes a Christian ruler. In a move that shows his educational and knightly progress from thinking that knights were God (281-84) to being part of institutionalized Christianity, before Percival leaves his court to go in search of his mother, he asks for a priest to say Mass (1806-8). He meets, fights, and slays the sultan's giant younger brother in a revealing comedy of errors—the giant had come into possession of Percival's ring given to him by his mother. The giant, in his comic attempt to woo Percival's mother, presents her with Percival's lost ring which prompts the widow's grief and madness over the supposed death of her son (2135-64). With the local Saracens in the romance so defeated, Percival's relationship to his mother restored, and the plot neatly tied up, the poem ends with Percival going on crusade:

> Sythen he went into the Holy Londe,
> Wane many cites full stronge,
> And there was he slayne, I undirstonde;
> Thusagatis endis hee. (2281-84)

Like Degrevant and some of the survivors of Malory's *Morte*, Perceval ultimately finds his end in the Middle East. Even if the romances do not linger on crusades, Saracens, or the Holy Land, a majority of the Arthurian canon's relationship to Saracens and the Middle East seems to be incidental, a way to build knightly reputation and credibility. It seems that when all else fails, the already Christian knight-hero can always chase the ultimate reward of martyrdom in the Holy Land. Considering this limited engagement—mere mentions of the Middle East, cardboard stereotypes of Saracens—the depth and complexity of Malory's Palomides stands out. Studying these texts is important because they create a tradition of Saracens in Arthuriana, but they also utilize a common trope. One of the things that makes the *Morte* interesting is not that it includes the knights going off to die in the Holy Land, but that Palomides is not. He is not one of the knights who goes on crusade, even though we know he survives. It seems strange that Palomides mostly disappears from the text after his conversion, and we do not know what happens to him. The last reference of Palomides is the end of "The Vengeance of Sir Gawain" where Lancelot makes Palomides the lord of Provence (700). For the Saracen knight who also fought on Lancelot's side when the Round Table began to fracture, one would think that Malory would mention him at the end of the romance as one of the crusaders—after all, he spends most of his story arc fighting for Christianity and dying on crusade would be the most fitting end.

Palomides and Religion

Christian knights are not the only ones willing to put their lives on the line for the Christian God—most of Palomides's story arc is about his relationship with religion. One of the most interesting qualities about Palomides is his dangerous religious liminality. For most of the "Book of Tristram," Malory's premier Saracen knight exists in the twilight zone of the spiritually stateless, meaning that Palomides is both Saracen and Christian, and yet, he is neither because he has not officially chosen. He is Saracen by birth, but fights for the Christian faith, even as he delays his baptism. Malory uses his unconverted status as a tool to heighten dramatic tension. One recurring element of his narrative is the real danger posed by Palomides's spiritual liminality. In one of the earlier episodes when Tristram battles against Palomides to rescue the abducted Isode, Isode asks Tristram to spare Palomides's life because he has not converted to Christianity yet: "And yet hit were grete pyte that I sholde se sir Palomydes slayne, for well I know by that the ende be done sir Palomydes is but a dede man, bycause that he is nat crystened, and I wolde be loth that he sholde dye a Sarazen" (Malory 267). Although Isode has no feelings for Palomides, as a Christian she is distressed at the thought that he should die without being converted. Her concern is not idle; she knows he is open to the possibility of conversion, because converting to Christianity for her sake was one of the things he offered her if she would consent to be his lover:

> And at that tyme sir Palomydes the Sarasyn drew unto La Beale Isode and profirde hir many gyfftys, for he loved hir passyngly welle. All that aspyde Tramtryste,[32] and full well he knew Palomydes for a noble knyght and a mighty man. And wete you well sir Tramtryste had grete despite at sir Palomydes, for La Beale Isode tolde Tramtryste that Palomydes was in wyll to be crystynde for hir sake. Thus was ther grete envy betwyxte Tramtryste and sir Palomydes. (Malory 239)

---

[32] Tramtryste is Tristram in disguise. Disguise features very heavily in Malory's "Book of Sir Tristram de Lyons" and for a while Tristram seeks to hide his identity by switching his name around (VIII: 242-3)

Palomides is willing to convert for Isode's sake if she will have him as her lover. Isode, however, does not show Palomides any favor or encouragement, thus relegating him to the position of being her devoted lifelong stalker, as Bonnie Wheeler notes (76). However, it is worthwhile to note that he does not, in fact, convert to Christianity for the love of Isode. Like the Saracen princesses who all appear to convert to Christianity for the assured access to their lovers instead of through any actual feeling for Christianity, Palomides initially dangles the option in front of Isode as a concession he is willing to make to have her. His conversion is conditional to her agreement to be his lover. Although, since access is not assured (she is already married to one man and the lover of another already Christian knight, Tristram) nothing ultimately comes from this offer. When Palomides does officially convert, it is on his own terms and for himself and faith instead of for another person. This distinction moves him from the company of literary female Saracen lovers[33] and puts him in the company of other converted Saracen knights like Ferumbras and Otuel. Palomides reinforces the gendered manner of textual conversions: Saracen women for love of Christian men, Saracen men for love of Christian God and worship. However, it is interesting to note that throughout the *Morte Darthur*, while Palomides exhibits a reluctance to convert impulsively, he does not espouse or exhibit any Islamic behaviors except that he calls himself a Saracen. He even professes to believe in Christianity: "I woll that ye all knowe that into this londe I cam to be crystyned, and in my harte I am crystyde" (Malory 408) but he refuses to simply convert even though he has decided to. The reluctance is puzzling and never entirely explained; other literary Saracens knights who convert do so quickly, but Palomides delays his own

---

[33] Discussed in more detail in Chapter 2

conversion by setting a seemingly arbitrary condition on his conversion: seven true battles for Christ (Malory 408).

Palomides spends his entire career measuring his worth against other knights; indeed, he tries his best to be a worthy knight, believing that knighthood is a profession where a good reputation is not granted but earned. Palomides applies the same ideology about knighthood to his own salvation, so it makes sense that he should feel as though he needs to "earn" the right to be Christian and to be a part of the Christian community as well. The idea of earning Christianity through battles for Christ's sake seems admirable, but it does tend to miss the basic idea of conversion: technically, he does not have to do anything more than believe and take baptism to be a full member of the Christian community. Throughout the "Book of Sir Tristram," the Christian community around him encourages him to get baptized. His reluctance to take the final step is never fully explained. Not once does the text indicate that Palomides would be unwelcome. Palomides even appears to consider himself unofficially Christian, even going so far as to tell two opponents in the Red City when they try to intimidate him that, "'Hit may well be,' seyde sir Palomydes, 'but as yet I wolde nat dye or that I were full crystyned. And yette so aferde am I nat of you bothe but that I shall dye a bettir Crystyn man than ony of you bothe. And doute you nat,' seyde sir Palomydes, 'ayther ye other I shall be leffte dede in this place'" (437). While Palomides does refer here to someday winning his battles and officially becoming Christian (with all the implications of him long outliving the both of them in the process), the sentiment here is that he is confident he will live to see that day. This reinforces what Malory has already told us: "And though he were nat crystyned, yet he belyved in the beste maner and was full faythefull" (436). Palomide's future turn to Christianity is assured throughout his story arc and no one who knows about him and his vow for the seven battles questions his resolve. If anything, the Arthurian community, like Malory's audience, are placed in the same position of rooting for him to succeed in his mission.

One possible explanation for Palomides's willingness to inhabit the liminal space between Christian and Saracen and somehow being both and neither at the same time, could be that Palomides expects a tangible, real-world trade-off—merely sacrificing his Saracen-ness for the sake of his soul is not enough. As Armstrong writes, "He worships at the altar of Arthurian knighthood" (191). The text never mentions if he values his Saracen identity, but he knows well the value others place on his setting his Saracen-ness aside and taking up the mantle of Christianity. It is a possibility that his reluctance could mean that he still has difficulty letting go of his identity, but the text does not support this reading. Rather, he wants a reward: preferably Isode's love, but he cannot have that. Therefore, he turns his attention to gaining acceptance into the wider knightly community as an equal. Sue Ellen Holbrook argues,

> Palomides holds a distinctive view of adult religious conversion for the social estate of knighthood: conversion must consist of inward desire…and a voluntary commitment to certain achievements appropriate to this estate before the ultimate goal of baptism can be fulfilled. This conception of chivalric commitment resembles the service a knight pledges through a vow. (85)

In other words, Palomides seems to conflate Christianity with good Arthurian knighthood. For him, knighthood is empty if it is devoid of deeds and the commitment to uphold the institution, and he treats conversion the same way. He vows service to God the way he would vow service to King Arthur. The reasons for conversion given by other Saracen-turned-Christian heroes do not move Palomides. Merely believing or professing to believe in Christian doctrine and deciding to convert because of feeling (Firumbras), or because he has witnessed a miracle (the Sultan of Damascus in *The King of Tars*), or even ultimately to have a lover (unless the lover is Isode) is not what ultimately moves him. His primary motivation (after Isode) is to succeed at knighthood, and he treats conversion as an extension of what it means to be a good knight. Palomides feels he must loudly and publicly prove his feeling and the truth of his conversion through feats of arms: "Thus, his conversion—like his knighthood—is an exaggerated performance: he attempts to out-Christian the other knights, as it were" (Armstrong 196). When Palomides converts, all participants in the baptism and the audience of the romance knows he means it. He has spent the entire "Book of Tristram" proving his dedication to the cause, even at his own great spiritual peril. Ultimately, it demonstrates Palomides's complete trust in God: he trusts that God will preserve him and allow him to fulfil his vow, a hope he verbalizes: "And I truste that God woll take myne entente, for I meane truly" (Malory 408).

Palomides is far from the only Saracen in Malory, but only once does he encounter another Saracen, a knight called Corsabryne. The entire episode is short, but there are a couple points of interest regarding the two knights. I argue that Corsabryne is a mirror for Sir Palomides—he reflects similarities in terms of both being unconverted Saracens as well as their aborted misadventures of being in love with indifferent women. Corsabryne serves as an illustration of the spiritual consequences that will occur if Palomides is slain prematurely, and he also reflects Sir Palomides's own failures in love and the consequential frustrations that follow. The text does not mention if Corsabryne is willing to convert to Christianity for his lady, or at all. In fact, far from proffering gifts and promising conversion, Corsabryne has a very different method of wooing his lady. He tells everyone who will listen that she is deranged so no one else will want to marry her: "he loved the damesell and in no wyse wolde suffir her to by maryed. For ever this Corsabryne noysed her and named her that she was oute of her mynde, and thus he lette her that she myght nat be maryed" (Malory 406). Naturally, the lady in question refuses to marry him. She objects to her good name being besmirched and her sanity being questioned. In fact, he becomes so persistent in his unwelcome attentions that she reaches out to Sir Palomides and requests he fight on her behalf, promising him marriage and her inheritance if he slays Corsabryne (406). This has the interesting implication that it is not Corsabryne's Saracen-ness that she objects to because she is completely willing to marry Palomides; it is just Corsabryne and his persistent slandering ways that makes him unappealing.

Palomides's defeat and beheading of Corsabryne is quick, but the aftermath is horrific: "And therewithall cam a stynke of his body, whan the soule departed, that there myght nobody abyde the savoure. So was the corpus had away and buryed in a wood, bycause he was a paynym" (Malory 407). Until now, Palomides's unconverted liminality seemed an abstract issue, but Malory heightens the dramatic tension by suggesting the consequences of dying while still a Saracen. This is the fate that will befall Palomides if he dies before christening. Corsabryne's death is particularly interesting if considered in the light of sainthood. Although there is a rather lengthy and involved process to being canonized a saint,[34] one of the accepted miracles that can help the case is if the deceased body "expels a sweet odour instead of the normal posthumous odours" (Melimopoulos and Nigmatulina). Corsabryne's decapitated body immediately exudes an odor so terrible that no one can abide it, suggesting the spiritual filth caused by his unconverted status affects his body as well. The text presents Corsabryne as literally rotten to the core. And if that is not terrible enough, the knight is denied proper burial: he does not receive funeral rites or a place

---

[34] See Allen Dudley Severence's "Beatification and Canonization with Special Reference to Historic Proof and the Proof of Miracles" for more on the process of inferring sainthood.

on hallowed ground. Although the text does not give many details, it seems to suggest that his body was buried quickly, probably in an unmarked grave, out in the woods (Malory 407). Suddenly, Palomides's unconverted state is important. The consequences of dying a Saracen are no longer abstract, but visceral and very public. Armstrong writes, "This is of course truly dangerous because if he dies in one of these pre-baptismal battles, he will go straight to hell … Yet the more he tries to establish his right to belong, the clearer it becomes he never will" (196). Malory's audience is now positioned quite oddly in terms of allegiance—they are not meant to be hoping for the demise of a Saracen knight, they are meant to root for him to live, win his battles, and be saved. When the Haute Prince recommends immediate baptism following the odiferous death of Corsabryne, Palomides, with his usual stubbornness, declines and tells him that he has taken a vow to delay baptism until he has earned it (Malory 408). Considering that the audience has just seen what the fate of an unconverted Saracen looks like, this seems to be either a foolhardy or a brave decision. Palomides might consider himself unofficially Christian, but he has not been formally inducted into their community, and the text never quite lets the audience forget that the outcome could still be tragic.

Palomides and Love

Palomides enters the narrative as another contender for Isode's love, arguably more an equal rival for Tristram than Isode's own husband King Mark, particularly as Mark becomes progressively more cowardly over the course of the story. Mark hardly presents a sympathetic figure or virile competitor for Isode's love. In contrast to Mark, Palomides does present a legitimate threat to Tristram, at least on paper. As Maghan Keita writes, "Palomides embodies the characteristics of the true champion, and is, therefore, presented as a worthy adversary: in fact, the worthy adversary—worthy of the hand of Isolde" (69). While she is writing about the prose *Tristan*, this sentiment is the same in Malory, as Palomides harbors an unceasing and entirely unrequited love for Isode. He places his heart on Isode, who shows him no favor whatsoever. When another knight asks if his lady has ever loved him back, Palomides admits that no, she has not: "I never aspyed that she ever loved me more than all the world ded, nor never had I plesure wyth her" (Malory 467). Isode never encourages his attentions, and Palomides is painfully aware that she is indifferent to his existence, at least romantically.

However, Palomides never seeks out another woman as paramour. Even Tristram marries another woman, Isode of the White Hands (Malory 273), but Palomides never gives his love to another, more available woman. In his battle with the unscrupulous Saracen knight Corsabryne, the lady Palomides champions makes the standard offer of a reward for his service: "And anone she sente hym a pensell and prayed hym to fyght with sir Corsabryne for her love, and he sholde have her and all her londis, and of her fadirs that sholde falle aftir hym" (Malory 406). If Palomides wins the battle against Corsabryne, the lady promises herself and all her wealth and inheritance to him, an offer which he never takes up nor mentions again. He battles and beheads Corsabryne, reveals to everyone that he intends to fight seven true battles for Christ before officially converting to Christianity, and retires for the evening (Malory 407-8). The matter ends there, and neither Palomides nor the lady mention it again.

Interestingly, another lady who engages Palomides to battle for her sake does seem to have feeling for Palomides, but the feeling is unrequited: "And this damesell loved sir Palomydes as her paramour, but the booke seyth she was of his kynne" (Malory 401). Though the damsel and her suit disappear from the text, that one detail has some interesting implications. First, while the damsel loves Palomides there is no indication that Palomides returns her feelings—in fact, considering that she disappears from the text and Palomides remains entirely faithful to Isode, nothing comes of it and Palomides is as indifferent to all other women as Isode is to him. Second, "she was of his kynne" has an interesting racial implication. The woman who loves Palomides is related to him, presumably meaning that she is also a Saracen or once had been.[35] She is presented, in her brief time in the text, as a woman more amenable to Palomides than Isode because she sees him as the same, but that sameness through their kinship makes her unsuitable. Palomides is willing to defend ladies in combat if they ask him, but he does not appear to care much for any of them. There is one damsel that Palomides wins from the Haute Prince who is never named, and who seems to ride off with Palomides (401, 406). However, this damsel seems to function as a tournament prize, and disappears shortly afterward.

Regardless, these romantic misadventures highlight the fact that Palomides is generally unlucky in love. Having set his love on one woman, no other ones tempt him—and the one woman who genuinely wants to be his paramour is related to him and therefore is unattainable. Arguably, Palomides is one of the most faithful lovers in Malory. As Dulin-Mallory writes, "Regardless of rebuffs and failures, the Saracen never gives up his love of Isolt, nor does he ever take another lover. In this regard, he is much more faithful than his Christian better [Tristram] who is often impressed with the beauty of other ladies, once tries to abduct Segwarydes's wife, and eventually marries a different Isolt" (168). Even the other great lovers in Malory, Lancelot and Tristram, are not so faithful to their lovers as Palomides

---

[35] The text never specifies that the lady herself is a Saracen, but she has been read that way by Cecire (143). My own initial reading also assumed she was Saracen, although if one considers that Palomides is the last holdout in his family to convert, she may well be converted herself. There is not enough detail in the text to know definitively one way or another.

is to Isode. Lancelot, admittedly, is bewitched and tricked into believing that Elaine is Guinevere and consequently begets Galahad (a reversal of the Uther-Igraine situation that produced Arthur), and Tristram ultimately marries another woman. Meanwhile, Palomides never falters either by accident or on purpose.

His regard for Isode aside, Palomides also seems to have a very intense relationship with Tristram as well—his rival in the lists and in love. Palomides's relationship with Tristram is just as complex and emotionally fraught as Palomides's one-sided devotion to Isode. Palomides is simultaneously frustrated by Tristram's successes, while at the same time he admires and wants Tristram's respect and fellowship. In *Between Men: English Literature and Male Homosocial Desire*, Eve Kosofsky Sedgwick writes,

> [I]n any erotic rivalry, the bond that links the two rivals is as intense and potent as the bond that links either of the rivals to the beloved: that the bonds of 'rivalry' and 'love,' differently as they are experienced, are equally powerful and in many senses equivalent. For instance, Girard finds many examples in which the choice of the beloved is determined in the first place, not by the qualities of the beloved, but by the beloved's already being the choice of the person who has been chosen as a rival. In fact, Girard seems to see the bond between rivals in an erotic triangle as being even stronger, more heavily determinant of actions and choices, than anything in the bond between either of the lovers and the beloved. (21)

Sedgewick's analysis of the erotic love triangle holds true in terms of the relationship between Tristram-Isode-Palomides. Throughout the "Book of Tristram" Palomides's relationship with Tristram vacillates between extremes of admiration and antagonism. There is the oft-quoted scene where the disguised Tristram holds Palomides back from plunging into a fountain after the sword he flung in a fit of temper and asks Palomides what he would do if Tristram were within his grasp. Palomides's conflicted emotions are neatly encapsulated by his response: "'I wolde fyght with hym,' seyde sir Palomydes, 'and ease my harte upon hym. And yet, to say the sothe, sir Trystram ys the jantyllste knyght in thys worlde lyvyng'" (IX: 325). Palomides wants to fight and beat him, but at the same time he respects him and seems to want Tristram's fellowship almost as much as he wants Isode's. René Girard notes this in his essay "Deceit, Desire, and the Novel" when he writes, "true jealousy ... always contains an element of fascination with the insolent rival" (300). Palomides's jealousy of Tristram because of Isode's love manifests in a constant love/hate, friend/enemy tug of war. As Olga Burakov Mongan writes,

> Palomides's triangular relationship with Tristram and Isode shows that in fact the bond of rivalry linking Palomides to Tristram is as powerful as the bond that connects Palomides to Isode, at times even surpassing the heterosexual relationship in the way it effects Palomides's behavior. Though Malory chooses to place the tragic love affair of Isode and Tristram in the background of his narrative, he offers us instead a no less complex love-hate relationship between Palomides and Tristram, thus privileging a male-male tie over a heterosexual relationship. (74-75)

All this serves to highlight the intense relationship between the two knights. Throughout the entire text, Isode is unattainable. Palomides might treat her as his sovereign lady, but she is not even remotely interested in acting her part in the relationship. However, because she is resistant, Isode is also a safe option for Palomides to choose as sovereign lady. By placing his love on her publicly,[36] he is freed from having to act the chivalric lover to any other woman even when opportunities present themselves—he already has a sovereign lady who is indifferent to his advances. In modern parlance, Isode is Palomides's "beard." She is his safest option to love from a distance because she will never return his feelings. With Isode placed securely in the middle of the intense love triangle as his beard and a highly visible symbol of both knights' ostensible heterosexuality, Palomides is free to have equally strong feelings for Tristram as he does for Isode.

---

[36] Lancelot cautions him against revealing his love: "I se, for to say the sothe, ye have done mervaylously well this day, and I undirstonde a part for whos love ye do hit, and well I wote that love is a grete maystry, and yf my lady were here, as she is nat, wyte you well, sir Palomydes, ye schulde nat beare away worship! But beware youre love nat be discovered, for an sir Trystram may know hit, ye woll repente hit" (Malory 449). Of course, Lancelot is late to this party—pretty much everyone, including Tristram and Isode—are aware of Palomides's love for her. Palomides is not a subtle man.

For instance, at the end of the Tournament at Lonzep, Palomides is equally sad to part from both, not just Isode: "and ever he made the grettyst dole that ony man cowde thynke, for he was nat all only so dolorous for the departynge frome La Beall Isode, but he was as sorowful a parte to go frome the felyshyp of sir Trystram. For he was so kynde and jantyll that whan sir Palomydes remembyrd hym [thereof] he myght never be myrry" (Malory 465). Palomides is sorry to leave Isode's presence but seems equally distressed or even more so to leave Tristram. Palomides's regard for Tristram is demonstrated in another episode that is not discussed quite so often, specifically when Dynadan, Palomides, and Tristram are thrown into Darra's prison. Tristram is accused of killing three of Sir Darras's sons and wounding two more, so Darras imprisons all three knights and Tristram falls grievously ill (Malory 332-333). While in prison, Palomides alternates between railing against Tristram and being genuinely afraid that Tristram might die: "And every day sir Palomydes wolde repreve sir Trystram of olde hate betwixt them, and ever sir Trystram spake fayre and seyde lytyll. But whan sir Palomydes se that sir Trystram was falle in syknes, than was he hevy for hym and comforted hym in all the beste wyse he coude" (Malory 333). On the one hand, we might read Palomides's antagonism as him being forever bitter at Tristram, but I rather think we could read the scene as Palomides's attempt to motivate Tristram to recover and survive the illness. After all, Palomides himself is often motivated by failure. Weakness spurs him on to be stronger, failure makes him fight that much harder to win. It makes sense that he might well be trying to antagonize Tristram into better health, if only so Tristram can get revenge for all Palomides's relentless goading and irritation. Of course, no amount of upbraiding moves a person to good health. Tristram's condition worsens and both Dynadan and Palomides are distraught: "sir Trystram fyll sick, that he wente to have dyed. Than sir

Dynadan wepte, and so ded sir Palomydes, undir them bothe makynge grete sorrow. So a damesell cam in to them and founde them mournynge" (Malory 338). There is nothing else that Palomides can do when they are trapped in prison and no amount of goading or care will save Tristram. Far from rejoicing the potential death of his romantic and professional rival, Palomides reveals a surprising depth of feeling about Tristram because he is beside himself with distress. He mourns the loss of Tristram before he is even dead.

Their relationship culminates in Palomides's seventh and final battle for Christ and his subsequent baptism, with Tristram serving both as the final combatant and godfather. The two knights meet and in a quiet moment, Tristram finally asks why Palomides has not yet converted: "I mervayle greatly of one thynge, that thou arte so good a knyght, that thou wolt nat be crystynde, and thy brother, sir Saffir, hath bene crystynde many a day" (Malory 508). Palomides reiterates the vow he had taken to fight seven battles, and that while he believed in Christ, until he fulfilled his vow he could not be baptized. Incidentally, he only had one last battle left before his vow was complete (508). Tristram is delighted, and the two of them fight to a draw (510). In this moment, near the closing of "The Book of Tristram," they settle all their grievances with each other. Palomides ends their battle with an apology and a confession. For once not weeping and wailing, Palomides unburdens his soul and is prepared to convert:

> "As for to do thys batayle," seyde sir Palomydes, "I dare ryght well ende hyt. But I have no grete luste to fyght no more, and for thys cause," seyde sir Palomides: "myne offence ys to you nat so grete but that we may be fryendys, for all that I have offended ys and was for the love of La Beall Isode. And as for her, I dare say she ys pyerles of all other ladyes, and also I profyrd her never no maner of dyshonoure, and by her I have getyn the moste parte of my worshyp. And sytthyn I had offended never as to her owne persone, and as for the offense that I have done, hyt was ayenste youre owne persone, and for that offence ye have gyvyn me thys day many sad strokys (and som I have gyffyn you agayne, and now I dare sey I felte never man of youre myght nothir so well-brethed but yf hit were sir Launcelot du Laake), wherefore I require

you, my lorde, forgyff me all that I have offended unto you! And thys same day have me to the nexte churche, and fyrste lat me be clene confessed, and aftir that se youreselff that I be truly baptysed. And than woll we all ryde togydyrs unto the courte of kyng Arthure, that we may be there at the next hyghe feste folowynge." (Malory 510)

Because neither one beats the other in this last clash (that Tristram engages in as a favor to Palomides), Palomides is finally able to fully let go of his old identity—his inferiority complex, his rivalry with Tristram, his possessive love of Isode, and the last shreds of his self as a Saracen. The entire passage is a confession to the man, who, in Palomides's mind, he has wronged the most ("as for the offense that I have done, hyt was ayenste youre owne persone"). This is passage is vital for the resolution of his story. He must "be clene confessed" to a priest, but he is getting a head start on the reparation part of the sacrament of confession. He apologizes for years of strife and offense toward Tristram and swears he did Isode "no maner of dyshonoure." In fact, he seems to think he owes them; he mentions that it was because he loved and wished to please Isode that he was driven to fight so hard for worship and success. Palomides no longer sees Tristram as his romantic rival for Isode. By letting Isode go, Palomides can finally have a relationship with Tristram that is not clouded with romantic jealousy. This allows him to directly ask for the one thing he has wanted, truly, above all: acceptance. Palomides no longer wants to fight with Tristram; he wishes to be friends with Tristram, to be brothers-in-arms, equals without anyone in between them: ("that we may be fryendys"). He is finally at the place in his life that he can accept that they love the same woman, and yet Isode will never love Palomides back. Palomides's and Tristram's new bond is cemented when Tristram stands as Palomides's godfather. It's a tangible, official relationship Palomides could never have with the married and emotionally unavailable Isode. Cecire notes something similar when she writes,

> At the christening the men excise Isode from their relationship by implicitly accepting that they can both love her without it interfering with their love for each other. They thus open up the possibility of satisfying their common desire at once, 'togydyrs'. The Church facilitates their union, and Isode's arguments to Tristram preceding this episode suggest that she, too, is complicit in removing herself from this equation, allowing the men to stop seeing each other through her and instead gaze directly at one another. (152)

Palomides cannot have Isode as a paramour, but he can have Tristram as a friend, and seals their newfound permanent friendship by having Tristram stand in as a godfather at his baptism. The two of them can put years of irritation, fighting, and mutual jealousy behind them, at long last.

Palomides and Gender

Malory's Palomides is a study in characterization and nuance, but this does not mean that his character is completely free of the stereotypes which permeate the image of the Saracen, both in literature and in the imaginations of the audience—or indeed, Malory himself. This dissonance becomes most obvious in terms of gender and sexuality. Often, Palomides is coded feminine. There is a long tradition of feminizing non-Christians, especially Jews and Muslims. In his essay, "Becoming Christian, Becoming Male?" Steven F. Kruger writes,

> Islam and Judaism were closely connected to each other in medieval Christian imaginations, and each was strongly affiliated with 'heresy': indeed, Islam was often treated as a Christian 'heresy' and Judaism often linked to 'heretical' conspiracies. From a Christian perspective, both these alternative religious traditions involved, like 'heresy,' a certain disturbance of gender. (21)

This disturbance of gender is best understood through the process of circumcision; there was a fundamental misunderstanding of circumcision by Christians as a loss of masculinity and virility at best, as a kind of castration at worst. This idea carried over into the way the West thought of the virility of their Eastern enemies. Kruger points out that, "Western European Christian discourses tended to construct Muslim and Jewish men as failing to live up to the 'masculine' ideals in the public realm, specifically in the realm of warfare" (22). Kruger also argues that many medieval texts seem to suggest a correlation between the feminization of Eastern men and the masculinization of their women (24). In this, the Eastern, non-Christian men are doubly damned: not only are they emasculated by physical circumcision and their ideological adherence to "heresies," but they also lack complete control over their women in the public sphere. In terms of the works examined in this dissertation, that stereotype was clearly a common one: both Josian and Floripas demonstrate masculine behaviors in battle and stratagems, and part of their conversion process is learning how to be "good Christian women" and thereby giving up their authority and autonomy to their Christian knightly lovers. This process is part of the allegedly transformative powers of Christianity and are common themes in the medieval romances I have discussed: Christianity tames wild Eastern women (*FER*, *Bevis*), has the power to white-wash a black Sultan (*KT*), and its absence even influences the nature of a corpse as demonstrated by the beheading and resultant foul odor of Corsabryne's body, the implication being that Islam befouls and Christianity sanctifies (*Morte Darthur*). In his essay, Kruger wonders if conversion has a gendered influence on the body and points out the problematic gender politics that comes from feminizing the Other in general. After all, the process of conversion requires converts, even the male converts, to submit (a feminine virtue) to the patriarchal hierarchies and authority of the Church (28).

Malory incorporates this stereotype in his portrayal of Palomides. Palomides is emotionally turbulent, forever frustrated or grieving his losses in love or prowess. Bonnie Wheeler writes, "Grief often begins with a ritualized self-mutilation that culminates for men in revenge and for women in despair" (66) and continues by arguing that Palomides's failure "causes him profound anguish, a form of self-castigating and specifically male grief required by the compulsory regimes of chivalry" (68). I am not sure I completely agree with this argument. If grief culminates in revenge for men, how can Palomides—forever the runner up, the firmly fourth best of knights (he is promoted up the ranks only when Lamorak is murdered)—really get revenge for his perceived loss of worship? The answer is that he cannot. He never maintains his spot at the top of the lists. He cannot beat or kill Tristram for Isode's love. He vacillates between hate/love and envy/grief so much that he becomes emotionally unstable, even to the point of surprising himself. He weeps and wails to the point where Malory describes him as crazy (464). At one point, his grief is so immense because he has lived in close quarters with Tristram and Isode for two months and made himself ill with pining. He catches sight of his reflection in a well and is appalled at the change in his appearance (Malory 473). His ultimate reaction to his continual losses (or perceived losses) is despair, and he frequently gives into it before rallying and trying to win again.

If outlets of grief are gendered active for men (revenge) and passive for women (despair), Palomides exists somewhere in the middle, and usually has far more in common with the feminine side of grief than he does with the masculine—especially since his attempts at enacting masculine grief typically result in more failure (or very temporary successes he cannot defend) which compounds his distress. And if Palomides is memorable for any other reason than he is a Saracen, it is for his repeated emotional breakdowns. Cecire writes about Palomides's struggle with Malorian masculinity. As an outsider, and particularly a Saracen outsider who is reluctant to convert, Palomides becomes the orientalist stereotype of the feminized Easterner:

> The association of the Other—particularly the 'Oriental' Other—with the feminine is now well established, and this trope often found expression in medieval literature...Palomydes's inability to win La Beale Isode and defeat Sir Tristram limits his knightly renown; his many attempts and failures result in depression and

> frustration that balance the threat that his knightly skill poses to the supremacy of Western Christianity. As a Saracen, an unwanted lover, and a defeated knight—and as a character emotionally influenced by these shortcomings—Palomydes is 'unmanned' in Malorian society. (Cecire 141)

Palomides cannot seem to make a win stick in any category, and throughout the text he is demonstrably unbalanced by it. Failure gets to him in a way that does not seem to bother other knights. Sir Dynadan, for example, is not nearly as motivated as his knightly friends to great deeds of honor and prowess, and generally approaches the travails of knighthood with more caution. In fact, Dynadan once tells Trystram bluntly that he wants no part in a particular fight because he fears he will be injured while trying to keep up with a superior knight: "For onys I felle in the felyshyp of sir Launcelot as I have done now with you, an he sette me so a worke that a quarter of a yere I kept my bedde. Jesus defend me … frome such two knyghtys, and specially frome youre felyship" (Malory 313). Dynadan recognizes his own limits. He might admire his friends (while strongly implying that they are reckless to the point of foolishness), but he feels no desire to even attempt to match them in deeds, especially since the one time he tried got him injured and bedridden for the better part of three months in recovery. Palomides has more ambition and is not as cognizant of his own limitations. In fact, Malory has Isode step in to save him from Tristram, which does not help matters. As Cecire writes,

> in Malory, Isode spares Palomydes out of pity and Christian generosity. This alteration does not only reduce Palomydes's prowess to make him a less serious threat than he is in the Prose *Tristan*, but also places Palomydes in the position of needing to be rescued by a lady. Such feminization of the Oriental Other heightens Tristram's masculinity by comparison and reminds the reader of Christian European dominance, martially, sexually, culturally and religiously. (145-6)

Palomides is stuck in between: between his Saracen identity and Christian aspirations, between thwarted knightly masculinity and despairing femininity, and between sanity and madness.

However, perhaps we fall into the same trap that Palomides does regarding his accomplishments. Palomides is something of an unreliable narrator; he is far from a mediocre knight. In *Gender and the Chivalric Community in Malory's Morte D'Arthur*, Dorsey Armstrong considers Palomides a "nontraditional knight" who challenges and offers alternatives to typical ideas of Western European knighthood (113). Palomides, Armstrong continues, "offers our first sustained view of a non-Christian knight in the *Morte D'Arthur*, although when we encounter him in the text he is always on his way to baptism" (143). The Arthurian community does not stand in his way but encourages him on his journey to baptism. However, though he might seem non-traditional, in some ways Palomides is like the whitened Saracen princesses who are already physically like the European Christian community they inevitably join: "Palomides is a significant character, but he is virtually indistinguishable from other Christian knights and, ultimately, converts to Christianity. Palomides, unrequited in his love for Isode, is ameliorated as a military or religious threat via his eventual absorption into the Christian culture" (Roland 37). Palomides is indistinguishable from other Christian knights because he acts like them and believes like them. Malory must keep referring to Palomides as a Saracen, just to remind his audience that despite all behavior evidence to the contrary, Palomides is Other. After all, as Hoffman notes,

> While we might not have a physical description of him [Palomides] (or of anyone else in Malory), he is clearly not inscribed with any visible, physical difference. Skin color is never mentioned, nor is any other feature that to a medieval or early modern audience would mark him as Middle Eastern or North African or anything else different from the English and Cornish knights in whose midst he operates. (49)

Hoffman thinks that one possible reason why no other description of Palomides is given is because the audience may already have a stereotyped image of a Saracen in mind that would suffice: "The image of the Saracen Malory expects his readers to imagine may, in fact, depend on the character of the Saracen in question. Bad Saracens look different; good

Saracens look, well, white. Thus, the apparent neutrality of the lack of specificity becomes a subtle endorsement of Western European normativity" (50). In other words, Hoffman believes that Malory uses common stereotyping tactics as a kind of imagery shorthand. Cecire seems to agree this is the case when she writes, "the fact that Sir Palomydes's identity as a Saracen precedes him so that he is often named or introduced as 'Sir Palomydes the Saracen' makes it important to consider him in terms of the Arabic associations of this designation" (140). Although, I must also point out that Malory does not seem to describe anyone's physicality except in the vaguest of terms. Because of the constant reminder that he is a Saracen, Palomides might well turn out to be Malory's best-described character after all.

In any case, the single time Malory does give us a physical description of Palomides, the result is unsatisfactory and raises more questions than it answers. After residing for two months at the Joyous Garde with Tristram and Isode, and pining away all the while, Palomides sees his reflection in the well: "anone he loked into the well and in the water he sawe his owne vysayge, how he was discolowred and defaded, a nothynge lyke as he was" (Malory 473). He recoils from the reflected image of himself because he looks ill and faded, but that does not necessarily give us a clear image as to what he looks like when he is hale and healthy. Although, the phrase "nothynge lyke as he was" might contain a clue. This might well be the closest to an actual physical description: "discolowred and defaded" does seem to imply that ordinarily he is not necessarily a pale man. If he is a swarthy man, then it makes sense that he would be shocked to see the way lovesickness and the grief of unrequited feelings have bleached and drawn his appearance with visceral signs of illness. He does not recognize his own reflection; in this moment, Palomides realizes with some horror that in his grief he has become Other to himself and he compares what he was to what he has become: "Why arte thou thus defaded, and ever was wont to be called one of the fayrest knyghtes of [the] world? Forsothe, I woll no more lyve this lyff, for I love that I may never gete nor recover" (473). This scene is the instant when Palomides has a hard but cathartic emotional realization about his current relationships with Tristram and Isode. In this moment, his reflection is not representative only of his physicality but also of his state of mind, and his recognition that his unresolved feelings are not healthy or good for him, and he is not ever going to achieve his goals of being the best knight and Isode's lover. He acknowledges to himself the futility of his pining. Over the course of his adventures, Palomides has changed as a knight and as a man, and for the first time he thinks that perhaps he has not changed for the better. Interestingly, this moment comes towards the end of his story arc—faced with the evidence of his reality, Palomides understands he should let his hopes for Isode go.

Palomides's liminality is clearly not limited to his spiritual statelessness. He is also liminal in terms of love. He loves a woman who does not love him back, and he wants the fellowship of knights, even as he wants the worship that comes from beating them in single combats and tournaments. He admires and loves Tristram while at the same time he is intensely jealous of him. A major part of his character arc is concentrated on resolving these difficulties. But spirituality and love, interconnected as they are, are only two obstacles he must figure out: he still must find a way to fit into the knightly community as well.

Palomides and the Chivalric Community

In this final section, I will examine Palomides and the seemingly impossible ideals of knighthood, in part by looking at the commentary of the others around him on his performance—from chastisements about knightly mistakes to compliments and esteem others have for him, even when he is not around to hear. In many ways, Palomides is held to a higher standard by the chivalric community and demonstrates how layered and difficult the knightly ideal is to attain and maintain. Throughout most of his narrative, Palomides is consistently inconsistent—one moment he might garner the admiration of the masses, and the next he might lose it through his own actions. Even in a text known for complex treatments of honor and what it means to fully participate in the chivalric community, Sir Palomides exhibits an extraordinary amount of psychological realism. Scholars have noted that Palomides is one of Malory's most complex and multidimensional characters, and certainly one of the most intricate portrayals of a literary Saracen in medieval literature in general.[37] Dulin-Mallory calls Malory's version of Palomides, "without question the most complex and interesting of any literary Saracen of the period" (165). There are episodes where Palomides almost seems like a villain, when he tricks others or behaves in a discourteous fashion that breaks the social rules of Arthurian knighthood. Unlike other knights, Palomides is not allowed to get away with misbehavior. After all, Gawain and his brothers (excluding Gareth), murder Lamorak and face no noticeable consequences. Palomides so much as toes the line of impropriety and the Arthurian community takes him to task on it. Palomides demonstrates how hard the knightly ideal is to achieve and maintain, as well as the mental and emotional toll such a pursuit has on a knight.

Perhaps part of the gatekeeping is because, as a Saracen, Palomides is an outsider. The Arthurian community does not appear to hold his Saracen-ness against him overtly, perhaps because they all know that he plans to convert after he earns his baptism through seven battles, but it is possible that discrimination comes out in other micro-aggressions. This would explain why Palomides is held to a higher standard. He is still Other, and even if he

---

[37] See also "Between Knights" by Olga Burakov Mongan, and "To the Well" by Sue Ellen Holbrook.

wants full access to the Arthurian community, Palomides is always on the outside looking in, a position which does not appreciably change even though he eventually converts. Moreover, if he wants to truly integrate into the community, he will have to learn all the rules and etiquette. Perhaps underneath it all, the Arthurian community is not as accepting as they initially seem, because they are intolerant of his mistakes. In the essay "Postcolonial Palomides," Dorsey Armstrong writes,

> The liminal figure of Palomides disrupts the fantasy of wholeness and inclusiveness that undergirds the organizational scheme of Arthur's kingdom and its knightly agents. The outsider tentatively invited in, who identifies his heritage as inferior and longs to replace it with that of the dominant culture, Palomides is a colonized subject, though not, in the geographical sense, a subject of colonialism. (179-180).

In other words, Armstrong argues that Palomides is key to understanding the dynamics of the Arthurian world from the point of view of someone who wants nothing more than to be an accepted, full member of the Round Table and never quite manages. As soon as Palomides does take that final step to become part of their order (baptism into the Christian faith), Malory sends him back to the outer fringes of the narrative. After an entire story arc about Palomides's desire to be a full member of the Arthurian community, the moment he removes what is ostensibly the last barrier—religion—to that membership, he returns to the wild Questing Beast chase and nothing ultimately comes of his new identity. He is a member of the Round Table in name, not necessarily in practice or politics. Ultimately, we might assume that Palomides's long bid for complete inclusion fails.

Palomides constantly tries to live up to the unrealistic models of knighthood set by his primary rivals, Lancelot and Tristram, but he continually faces the frustration of never quite measuring up to them in terms of prowess, love, faith, or even masculinity. He is not the best knight, but he is far from a mediocre one. For Kevin Grimm, Palomides is the embodiment of extremes of knightly love/attraction and envy. Palomides spends most of his story arc torn between wanting the fellowship of good knights and wanting to be the best of them with the most prowess and worship (69). However, for Palomides, these two desires—fellowship and ultimate worship—often prove incompatible. His competitive drive to be the best of knights often puts him at jealous odds with the very knights he wants to befriend, and sometimes even himself. In her essay "Grief in Avalon: Sir Palomydes' Psychic Pain," Bonnie Wheeler writes,

> Like his chivalric friends, most scholars are drawn to Sir Palomydes as The Knight Thwarted, the hopeless knight. The promise of chivalry is that men who win through physical prowess on the battlefield will receive their chosen lady as booty, and chivalric literature celebrates the beauty of the males' romantic/martial quest. The chivalric story of Sir Palomydes as almost-best details the frustrating loss all men must experience so that the chosen few might succeed. Malory complicates our views of chivalric masculinity through Sir Palomydes, so this thwarted knight projects the blight as well as the glamour of chivalry. (73)

Palomides has ambitions of being the best and reacts with frustration when he is never even second best. The moment that best encapsulates Palomides's frustrations and thwarted desires happens during the tournament at Lonezep. At the tournament, Palomides is doing exceptionally well, a performance which even prompts king Arthur to remark on his prowess: "So God me helpe ... he is a passynge goode knyght" (462). Yet, just moments later, Tristram takes the field. With the crowd chanting Tristram's name as their favorite champion, Malory writes one of the most devastating lines regarding Palomides: "And than was sir Palomides clene forgotyn" (463). That single sentence is the summation of Palomides's entire career, at least in his own mind.

Still, as mentioned above, Palomides is often held to a higher standard—or is instructed on proper knighthood by the Arthurian community whenever he fails. Palomides's mishaps are quickly noted and commented upon by others, most notably Lancelot, Tristram, Isode, and Arthur. He clearly has the prowess to be an excellent knight, but he sometimes falls short when interpersonal skills such as generosity or courtesy are needed to best interact with ladies and other knights. In this way, he illustrates the multifaceted nature of knighthood: it is not enough to be an accomplished fighter, but there are also standards of ethics and social behavior that must be observed. Palomides does not always pass muster. There are two scenes that mirror each other in a fascinating way: both scenes involve the death of a horse during a tournament, but the behavior modelled in each is different. In the first scene during the tournament of Surluse, Palomides and the Haute Prince, Sir Galahalte, are locked in combat and Galahalte's sword slips: "sir Galahalte smote a stroke of myght unto sir Palomydes sore uppon the helme; but the helme was so harde that the swerde myght nat byghte, but slypped and smote of the hede of his horse" (Malory 401). Galahalte is horrified. Immediately he stops fighting, dismounts, apologizes to Palomides, and offers his own horse as recompense. By contrast, in the second scene, Palomides kills Lancelot's horse intentionally to gain the advantage over the much bigger and more accomplished knight. The resulting outrage from the onlooking crowd and knights is palpable:

> Than was the cry huge and grete, how sir Palomydes the Saresyn hath smyttyn downe sir Launcelots horse. Ryght so there were many knyghtes wroth wyth sir Palomydes bycause he had done that dede, and helde there ayenste hit, and seyde hyt was unknyghtly done in a turnemente to kylle an horse wylfully, other ellys that hit had bene done in playne batayle lyff for lyff. (Malory 449)

The differences between the two scenes are a study in proper knighthood. In the first scene, Galahalte makes reparations immediately and without prompting, because killing a knight's horse—even accidentally—is a very expensive transgression. Palomides responds, "I thanke you of youre grete goodnes, for ever of a man of worship a knyght shall never have disworshyp" (401). Galahalte models good knightly behavior: he has done someone wrong and addresses it sincerely and generously. When it is Palomides's turn, he does not. For one, he does not apologize until he is literally unhorsed by another knight (Ector de Marys), at

Lancelot's swordpoint, and realizing that he is facing a very angry Lancelot. Perhaps "apologize" is the wrong word because while he throws himself on Lancelot's mercy, he does not actually say he is sorry or offer reparation:

> 'A, mercy, noble knyght,' seyde sir Palomydes, 'of my dedis! And, jantyll knyght, forgyff me myne unknyghtly dedis, for I have no power nothir myght to wythstonde you. And I have done so muche this day that well I wote I ded never so muche nothir never shall do so muche in my dayes. And therefore, moste noble knyght of the worlde, I requyer you the spare me as this day, and I promyse you I shall ever be youre knyghte whyle I lyve, for and yf ye put me from my worshyp now, ye put me from the grettyst worship that ever I had or ever shall have.' (Malory 449)

This is not one of Palomides's most shining moments. In fact, this scene comes directly after he has done marvelously that day at the tournament of Lonzep and everyone has admired his prowess and lamented that he is not Christian (448). This scene shows just how quickly the admiration of his fellow knights can turn against him because of a single mistake, how arduous building a good reputation is, and how quickly honor and worship can be lost through unknightly actions. For his part, Palomides admits that he has behaved in an unknightly manner: "forgyff me myne unknyghtly dedis." But nowhere in the above passage does he express any kind of remorse for his actions, nor does he offer his own horse as reparation as Sir Galahalte did for him. Instead, he offers to be Lancelot's knight for life and he asks Lancelot's mercy and forgiveness; failing that, he asks Lancelot not to "put [him] from his worshyp" or, in other words, Palomides has had one of the best days of his entire knightly career and he is asking Lancelot not to take it from him. If Lancelot decides to press the issue, Palomides will be publicly shamed and lose all the worship he has won that day. Palomides's only concern in this moment is himself, but Lancelot grants the favor Palomides asks of him: "I se, for to say the sothe, ye have done mervaylously well this day … sytthyn my quarell is nat here, ye shall have this day the worshyp as for me; consyderynge the grete travayle and payne that ye have had this day, hit were no worship for me to put you frome hit" (449). Lancelot acknowledges that he noticed that Palomides is having an exceptionally good day and allows Palomides to save face and keep his worship. Moreover, granting Palomides this request, Lancelot safeguards his own worship and gains an ally for life.

This is not the last time Palomides is reproved by another for unknightly misbehavior. There is another episode when Arthur decides to go and look at the beautiful Queen Isode (who is being escorted by Tristram and Palomides) so he dresses as a knight errant and sets out with a long-suffering Lancelot. Arthur ignores Palomides's order to withdraw and not bother Isode and so Palomides promptly unhorses Arthur (452). Tristram settles the quarrel and then tells Palomides that he behaved badly: "ye ded nat worshipfully when ye smote downe that knyght so suddeynly as ye ded. And wyte you well ye ded youreselff grete shame, for the knyghtes came hyddir of there jantylnes to se a fayre lady, and that ys every good knyghtes parte to beholde a fayre lady, and ye had nat ado to play such maystryes for my lady" (453). There is a lot in this passage to parse out. First, Tristram tells Palomides that he acted too quickly and recklessly—he did not know who he was engaging in combat and that can be dangerous. Of course, this is advice only loosely followed in the *Morte*, considering how many times friends and brothers duel with each other and only find out who the other combatant is at the last minute. Second, Tristram tells him that the knights came to marvel at Isode's beauty. This suggests that part of knighthood is not only a knight's relationship with a lady, but also his ability to turn an appreciative heterosexual gaze upon beautiful women, including beautiful women who do not belong to them. Third, Tristram reproves Palomides for overstepping his bounds: after all, Tristram is Isode's lover. If anyone should defend her in a battle, it should be Tristram, not Palomides.

A third notable instance where Palomides falls short of ideal knighthood is revealed in the way that the Arthurian community treats disguise. When knights are in disguise, it gives them the opportunity to win more glory and renown because they are engaging with opponents who do not know their identity. When they are incognito, their victories are based purely on their deeds and prowess, not their fame. Other knights are more likely to engage them in battle while disguised, where if others knew their true identities, lesser knights like Dynadan might defer to the more famous knight to avoid the shame of defeat, or to avoid possibly dealing a death-blow to one of the kingdom's best. Knights like Lancelot, Tristram, and even Arthur routinely hide their identity during tournaments and while they are riding errant across the countryside. In fact, Lancelot's tendency to disguise himself is so common that it becomes something of a joke:

> Than they all lokyd upon sir Launcelot and seyde,
> 'Sir, ye have begyled us all wyth youre covered shylde.'
> 'Hit is not the fyrst tyme,' seyde Kyng Arthure, 'he hath done so.' (Malory 352)

Arthur himself seems wryly amused and accustomed to Lancelot's antics in disguise. It almost becomes an in-joke—Lancelot often rides as an anonymous knight errant. Or, sometimes, Lancelot even appears in drag. During the tournament at Surluse, Lancelot's disguise habits helps him to play a joke on Dynadan when Lancelot dresses as a damsel and then goes out to the field: "sir Launcelot disgysed hymselff and put upon his armoure a maydens garmente freysshely attired. Than sir Launcelot made sir Galyhodyn to lede hym thorow he raunge, and all men had wonder what damsell was that" (410). Lancelot's disguise is enough to fool many of the onlookers, but Dynadan has a moment of consternation where he thinks it is Lancelot—and while he is distracted, Lancelot strikes him off his horse, dresses Dynadan in women's garments, and presents him to the Guinevere who laughs so hard she falls on the ground (410).

Palomides also uses disguises. He is incognito at the tournament of Surluse, although it is not a very good disguise: the image of the Questing Beast is on his shield and trappings (Malory 401). Later, during the tournament at Lonezep, Palomides courts trouble and disfavor by maliciously disguising himself to ambush Tristram: "Than sir Palomydes sawe that sir Trystram was disgysed, and thought to shame hym" (456). He asks an injured knight for his armor, saying that "myne ys overwell knowyn in thys fylde, and that hath done me grete damayge" (456-7). The only person who knows that Palomides is up to dastardly shenanigans is Isode who, "was wrothe oute of mesure wyth sir Palomydes, for she saw all his treson frome the bygynnge to the endynge" (459). Palomides knows the disguises that Lancelot and Tristram are currently using (although he pretends he does not know them) even if they do not know his. He allows the two knights to fight each other, with the hope that Lancelot will beat Tristram. Once his treachery is revealed, Palomides is reviled by the company for such behavior. Tristram accuses him of "grete unjantylness" (459) before forgiving him with his typical magnanimity, while an enraged Isode calls Palomides "a felonne and traytoure" (460) and tells Tristram that she saw Palomides intentionally deceive him. Even Arthur, when he hears of the misadventure, chastises Palomides: "that was unknightly done of you as of so good a knyght, for I have harde many people calle you a curtayse knyght" (461-2). Arthur's comment is especially cutting because the king acknowledges all the good things he has heard about Palomides throughout his career, has admired Palomides's prowess personally, and then personally witnesses evidence to the contrary.

The disapproval of the entire Arthurian community makes clear the etiquette about disguises: they are not to be used with malice, but Lancelot's trickery of Dynadan and

Palomides's trickery of Lancelot and Tristram are not treated the same. Both tricks are relatively meanspirited, but since Lancelot's trick is deemed funny and not deadly, he can get away with it, whereas Palomides is reprimanded. Lancelot's trick is acceptable because it is a joke within the community. In Chapter 1, I discussed the function of laughter and unlaughter to set boundaries and determine a community's sense of identity and ethics. Laughing at a joke, signals inclusion into community that the joke is meant for. A lack of laughter when laughter is expected (unlaughter), signals strong disapproval and removes the person(s) from the intended audience. Lancelot's joke on Dynadan, although mean, is community building. Even Guinevere laughs and appreciates the caper, and ultimately, no true harm comes to Dynadan, except to his pride. By contrast, Palomides's trickery could have had lethal consequences. Tournaments are dangerous enough because accidents can happen, but most of the knights are friendly or professionally courteous towards each other. Palomides's attempt to facilitate the harm or death of Tristram by way of Lancelot is a dishonorable abuse of disguise.

Palomides's complexity comes from his very human reactions to setbacks, adversity, and failures. He sometimes falls short of the seemingly effortless ideal knighthood embodied by Lancelot and Tristram. He has the skills and the physical prowess to be one of the best knights in the world, but the frustrations of not being able to surpass and maintain supremacy over his rival knights sometimes lead him to do unchivalrous acts against those knights. Palomides's hardest lesson is learning that half of being a good knight is being able to behave in a courtly, honorable manner, even when under duress.

Conclusion

Palomides is a complex feat of characterization in the *Morte Darthur*. Although Saracen characters are not unknown in Arthuriana, Malory's Palomides emerges as one of the best and most sympathetic portrayals of a Saracen in the whole Middle English romance tradition. Palomides is a character defined by constant struggle. Malory had many opportunities to make his premier Saracen knight a villain—and while Palomides does occasionally do borderline-villainous things, he remains a good knight who is relatable in his insecurities and frustrated desires to become one of the best knights. He gives the audience a good look at the underpinning of good knighthood: the personal and physical costs the profession demands, the frustrations of giving everything and falling short, and the grim reality that for every knight who becomes famous, there are many more who are not. Palomides demonstrates how difficult the knightly ideals are to attain; he must learn that prowess is only part of the equation, and that other virtues such as courtesy, generosity, and diplomacy are sometimes required to fit into the Arthurian community. Other knights make knighthood look easy. Palomides makes it look real.

Palomides's Saracen-ness allows him the space to do this better than any of the Christian knights. If the Saracen princesses discussed in the last chapter are given leeway to behave outside of what Western European Christianity considers acceptable for women, Palomides is granted a measure of the same freedom. The princesses must learn to become good Christian women, and Palomides must learn how to be a good Christian knight. Only when he has ostensibly learned this lesson is he able to convert to Christianity. It is not enough for him to merely set aside his Saracen nature. If he wants full inclusion into the Arthurian community, he must operate by all the same rules that the Christian knights do.

Otherwise, Palomides risks becoming a villain—another treacherous Saracen in the same vein as *Richard Coer de Lion*'s version of Saladin.

Despite Palomides's occasional knightly missteps, Malory uses his spiritual statelessness to heighten the drama. Audiences are meant to root for him to succeed, to survive his adventures and battles because if he does his conversion to Christianity is all but assured. He converts at the end of his tale, and finally seems to find some peace not just with himself, but also with his greatest rival Tristram, who he has loved and hated in equal measures throughout the entire tale. Palomides also has complicated relationships with Isode and the knights he wants to both beat and befriend. He constantly tries to be the best knight in the vain hope that Isode will notice him, and her indifference to him fuels his emotional turbulence. Malory uses Palomides to demonstrate what happens when courtly love is left permanently unrequited. Palomides must give Isode up eventually, because she is actively and consistently resistant to his overtures. Of course, his story feels unfinished. As soon as he converts, he leaves the narrative, only mentioned briefly in passing afterward. Once his story closes, we no longer have access to his inner thoughts—he loses all psychological realism and becomes just a familiar name on the page, one who haunts the fringes of Arthurian society and tournaments but never engages with audiences personally again. We do not know his exact fate, what changes—if any—Palomides undergoes post-conversion, or whether he cracks the social code of conduct that the rest of the knights seem to instinctively know. As soon as he converts and becomes like the rest of the Arthurian community, he loses everything that makes him unique.

Conclusion

Throughout this dissertation, I have examined ways that popular Middle English romance helps to build, shape, and maintain and English Christian identity through opposition with the Saracen Other. Each of the chapters explores at least one of my major research questions, as outlined in my introduction. My project also seeks to add to the ongoing conversations about the usefulness of postcolonial theory in medieval studies, and like Akbari, Calkin, and Heng, I consider the ways that the romances think about the Middle East and want to either control or consume it.

Chapter one primarily deals with the question: how do textual Saracens help build an English identity? To find answers, I studied *Richard Coer de Lion*, a romance which is primarily about identity. It is also a more complex romance than one may initially think because it builds and emphasizes English identity on the one hand, and on the other hand it also subverts that identity. The poet begins the romance promising to tell the audience a story about an English king to the English people, in the English language, and rewrites Richard's historically French lineage to match. Richard becomes an ambiguous character in the text: at once the figurehead for what it means to be English, while also possessing ostensibly non-English qualities, particularly a demonic nature because of his demon-mother, the princess of Antioch, Cassodorien. Throughout the romance, Richard has contact with many Saracens: some he consumes in place of pork, some he converts to Christianity, and Saladin. Each major encounter affects the representation of English identity. The cannibalism scenes imply that Richard, and by extension, the English as conquerors, will eradicate everything about the Saracens—even going so far as to consume them. Even the ones he converts are metaphorically consumed, their religion swallowed up by Christianity. And Saladin, historically Richard's equal in terms of strategic brilliance and warfare, is rewritten as a scheming coward to highlight romance-Richard's complete dedication to the crusade.

My second line of questioning considered female characters: how are female characters, both Christian and Saracen, used as instruments of colonialism in crusade romances? Moreover, how do they legitimize the crusades? In many popular crusade romances, women are secret weapons of conversion: either they are converted to Christianity themselves, or they facilitate the conversion of an entire nation to Christianity. Saracen princesses like Floripas and Josian convert to Christianity to marry their Western lovers, and often shield these knights from the harmful intentions of the princesses's own kin (Josian persuades her father not to punish Bevis for killing his knights; Floripas facilitates Guy's rescue from her father). By choosing Christian knights as their lovers and rejecting Saracen suitors, the Saracen princesses legitimize the crusade. They embody many Western fantasies, including the upward mobility of knights, male power, and the supremacy of Christianity. The Christian damsel of *The King of Tars* has a much harder job: she must go undercover in an enemy court and convert it from within. She marries the Sultan of Babylon and pretends to convert to his religion to save her people from war and is ultimately able to convert him to Christianity through miracles. Once he is Christian, they promptly plan the forced conversion of the entire nation. The Christian damsel is an ideological crusader—she does not have to personally take arms to colonize or defeat Saracens, she just must convert their leader. To an extent, even Cassodorien, although she falls into neither category, has a hand in legitimizing Richard's crusade because he gets Antiochian heritage from her.

Finally, I asked what it means to convert from one identity to another, or more specifically, how does a Saracen join the Christian community? My inquiry led me to examine Thomas Malory's Saracen knight, Palomides. Palomides demonstrates how difficult it is to join a new community. He struggles to be accepted as a man, a knight, and a Christian in the Arthurian community. While he might escape much of the overt prejudice against Saracens that is present in many Middle English romances, Palomides cannot shake more insidious racial and gender stereotypes: his constant emotional turbulence stemming from never quite measuring up to Lancelot and Tristram and his unrequited love of Isode haunt him throughout the text. However, Malory never makes Palomides a villain, even if he does behave unchivalrously from time to time. Palomides does not officially convert until the end of his story arc because he is not ready to be baptized. He can only become Christian when he has let go of his worldly concerns and anxieties. Unfortunately, almost as soon as he is baptized, Palomides mostly disappears from the text, except for a few brief appearances afterward, so we have no direct evidence of how well he integrates into the Arthurian community, but he does not seem to integrate completely: he resumes his pursuit of the Questing Beast and eventually takes Lancelot's side during the final fracturing of the Round Table.

    This dissertation is hardly an exhaustive examination of Saracens and their functions and importance in Middle English romances. Future expansions of this project into a manuscript would almost certainly include in-depth examinations of *Guy of Warwick*, *Sir Isumbras*, and the Constance tradition. There is a significant amount of work left to do with Middle English romances in general, but especially with the crusade romances that contain Saracens. In a post 9/11 world, these romances and their tropes resonate with audiences and they still appear in contemporary entertainment, albeit in different forms. Understanding the images of the Saracen, the colonial conflicts, and the willful misunderstanding of the Other that is present in Middle English romances may be key to understanding our treatments of the current images of the Saracen Other in our own orientalist popular culture romances. I use the word "Saracen" here instead of "Muslim" because contemporary American pop culture rarely engages with what it means to be Muslim in any meaningful way. Many Muslim, and even Jewish, characters in popular film and television are treated more like the monolithic medieval Saracen stereotype than as empathetic representations of real people (see: *NCIS*, and *NCIS: Los Angeles*, for examples). In short, understanding the representations of the Saracen and the colonial impulses of the West in medieval Middle English romance may be integral to understanding the roots of contemporary Western attitudes toward the Saracen Other.

www.ingramcontent.com/pod-product-compliance
Lightning Source LLC
Chambersburg PA
CBHW050314010526
44107CB00055B/2231